One of the hardest things to do is look at yourself honestly. And to do so without self-criticism—but with the passionate desire to improve your life for the sake of others—is even harder. Carlos Whittaker is a fitting guide for the journey. He will take you to the hard place and turn the light on. Nonsense living in the dark when a little light can create a more healthy, enjoyable life.

DONALD MILLER

In a world obsessed with outward appearances and dealing with the symptom, not the cause, it's wildly refreshing to see Los dip far below the surface to address the real spiders that cause the real pain in our very real lives.

JON ACUFF, *New York Times*
bestselling author of *Finish*

Carlos Whittaker has created a vehicle for all of us to better understand the aspects of our lives that prevent us from being free to grow and love without limitation. *Kill the Spider* is a masterpiece! I could not put it down. You won't ⸻ ⸻ either.

⸻ILTON

I really wish Carlos had not written thi⸻ ⸻ ⸻e had written a book called *Eat the Gumdrop* ⸻ ⸻rn, but he had the audacity to write *Kill the S*⸻ ⸻t just a book, it's a declaration of independenc⸻ ⸻aced his demons, the rest of us have no excuse ⸻ You need this; it won't feel good, but you need ⸻

LEVI LUSKO, bestselli⸻ ⸻ipe Right:
The Life-and-Death Power ot ⸻ *d Romance*

In *Kill the Spider*, Carlos not only takes us on his journey to defeat the lies that were holding him down but gives us practical advice as to how to kill the spiders in our own life. I really loved this book and will be handing out a ton of copies to my friends.

MIKE FOSTER

KILL THE SPIDER

Also by Carlos Whittaker

*Moment Maker: You Can Live
Your Life or It Will Live You*

KILL THE SPIDER

GETTING RID OF WHAT'S REALLY HOLDING YOU BACK

CARLOS WHITTAKER

ZONDERVAN

Kill the Spider
Copyright © 2017 by Carlos Enrique Whittaker

Requests for information should be addressed to:
Zondervan, *3900 Sparks Dr. SE, Grand Rapids, Michigan 49546*

ISBN 978-0-310-33800-0 (softcover)

ISBN 978-0-310-50004-9 (audio)

ISBN 978-0-310-33801-7 (ebook)

Published in association with the literary agency of The Fedd Agency, Inc., Post Office Box 341973, Austin, Texas, 78734.

Art direction: Curt Diepenhorst
Interior design: Denise Froehlich

First printing August 2017 / Printed in the United States of America

19 20 21 PC/LSCH 15 14 13 12 11 10 9

Heather—

These words are wrapped in your

wisdom and warfare.

My spiders never stood a chance.

CONTENTS

INTRODUCTION

My family recently moved to a new home on the south side of Nashville. "New" is probably a little misleading, but what can I say? It's new to us. Actually, it's a 1955 ranch-style home on a corner lot in a great neighborhood. I like the corner lot because that means more people can see how incredibly manicured I keep my lawn—way better than if I were living at the end of a cul-de-sac. (Yeah. I'm that guy.) Four bedrooms, three baths. A finished basement and a garage with a shop. Move over Cleavers. The Beaver's hood had nothing on Los's new hood.

We'd been in the house just a few months before we took off for a summer road trip, leaving the house to pet sitters and a few guests who needed a place to lay their heads as they passed through Nashville.

We were on a stretch of deserted highway in the middle of nowhere Wyoming when a friend staying at our house called Heather, clearly rattled. The panic in our friend's voice came through loud and clear even though I couldn't hear what was being said. I braced myself for the upcoming conversation where we'd have to tell our kids that their dog Pope had tragically died in some unfortunate set of circumstances.

"Really? Are you sure?" Heather asked our guest. "I've never seen one the entire time we've lived there. Okay. That's fine. Okay. Just tell me how much," Heather said in a calm cadence over the phone. What in the world were they talking about? Heather hung up the phone.

"Natalie said she saw a spider on her bed. She thinks it's a brown recluse," Heather explained. "She's kinda unnerved about it."

"There's no way it was a brown recluse. It was probably just a garden spider. Tell her to stay upstairs and out of the basement. It's no big deal. We will deal with it when we get back," I replied.

Fast forward four weeks. Road trip done. We pulled back into our driveway on the corner lot. Manicured lawn looks good. Life is good.

Immediate chaos commenced. Five Whittakers and 41,233 pieces of luggage. When we walked into the house it felt different than when we'd left. Not bad. Just different. When a home is lived in by five people on a daily basis, the smells from the kitchen, the dirt from the nine-year-old shoes, the chaos of the tweens' lives spills over everything. The house lacked the right smells, touches, and life. It was clean, but lonely looking. Ah, well. It'd be back to usual soon, I reasoned.

In the back of my mind was Natalie's run-in with that "brown recluse" spider. I still wasn't convinced that's what it was, but something about that cobweb had me peeking under every pillow.

"Change the sheets on your beds, kids," I yelled out. Funny how that spider sighting a few weeks earlier was suddenly bothering me more than it was when I was in Wyoming. As we settled into our evening rhythms, every-thing felt right. It smelled right. We had an incredible evening together, snuggling our 115-pound Bernese mountain dog and apologizing profusely for leaving him for so long. At the end of the night, Heather crawled in bed and was reading one of her Amish love-story novels. I was watching *Sports Center* in the living room and the kids were sucking up all the Wi-Fi they had been deprived of in the minivan. That's when I heard the scream. Not a yell, no, it was a scream. It came from my bedroom. I was halfway there when I saw Heather running and stripping off her pajamas. What in the world?!

"It's a spider! It was a spider on our bed, Carlos. *On our bed.* You have to find it and kill it. Go find it. I want to move. This is not okay. *Go find it. OMG,*" Heather spilled out.

I found the spider. It was a brown recluse. And it was on *my* bed. In a matter of five seconds, the most important thing in my life was ridding my home of spiders. Funny how I was fine putting a Band-Aid on the problem before, telling poor Natalie to just "move upstairs," and now I was ready to drop a nuclear bomb on my house to get rid of the problem.

I had a "spider guy" at my house by noon the next day, and extermination began. It was a month before we were free of spiders. We not only had to exterminate them, we had to fill any holes in the cracks of our walls, ceilings, and closets that they could sneak through.

"This summer heat has these recluses coming out into the open," the spider guy said. "Every neighborhood with houses like yours, built in the fifties are calling me. Everybody has spiders. It's just nobody does anything about it until they come out of hiding."

This exterminator just dropped a truth bomb.

The scenario at my house creeped you out, right? Good. It's kind of a metaphor for where I found my soul recently: freaked out, adrenaline rushing, blood pumping in my ears, feeling terrible and seriously abandoned, anxiety at an all-time high. And it had nothing to do with spiders in my home and everything to do with spiders in my heart.

Here's the thing: There was something sinister in my life—something I didn't even know was there—and it was threatening my life. It almost cost me everything.

Anyone who knows me will tell you: I love telling stories. So much so that I've found a way to do it for a living, speaking at conferences and churches, leading people in worship, and vlogging our family adventures on YouTube. Often my beautiful wife and three amazing kids come along and we just have great adventures, drinking deep of every drop of the good life. It's not a stretch to say I'm living the dream. What's not to love? I get to make a living pointing to the Good News—that God is here for us in every season of life no matter how you *feel*. He is right there. God animates my life, constantly extending grace and power to me, blessing me over and over again. And I get to tell people about this goodness—*for a living!*

And yet (comes the dreaded next line), not too long ago I woke up to the reality that I was stuck, repeatedly messing up. I was hurting people and bringing shame and stress on myself and my family, even while I was lifting up the name of Jesus, striving to live in communion with Him, and doing all I could think of to glorify the name of Jesus. Traveling the world, seeing that same Good News transform lives, I was still somehow doing destructive things and hurting the people I love most.

How is this even possible? How can a person lift up the name of Jesus with one hand and simultaneously destroy his own life with the other? Do you know what I mean? Have you been there? Can I get an amen? Have you ever thrown up your hands, wondering why in the world you keep feeling more like the prodigal son gone back to the hog pen and wishing you could eat their slop, even after you've already been welcomed back into your Father's arms? Have you ever wondered, "Why in the world do I keep making the same mistakes?" Maybe you've realized you have some addictive behaviors. Maybe fear has motivated your decisions more often than you'd like. Or—and this is a big one—maybe you know Jesus is your Savior, but somehow you still feel like you need saving. It's a never-ending battle, and you just can't win. People, this is the book for you.

Truth is, that's the perplexing mind-set I was in when something crazy happened. I had a pretty miserable, phenomenal, mind-blowing week on a farm just outside Nashville that turned into an epic mountaintop kind of experience. The kind of experience that changes a person from the inside out. The kind you can't help but share. That's why I'm coming clean, sharing my story. My story about hunting down the spider.

THE DRIVE

I figured I needed therapy. I mean, let's be honest, we all are a little bit crooked inside and could use some Yoda-like guidance on this journey called life. Personally, I had this recurring pattern of making the same sorts of bad decisions over and over again. So, of course, therapy was probably a good idea.

I had been a regular visitor in Al's office for months. We had taken the spotlight of grace and shined it on all my sins. We had uncovered glimpses of hope in war-torn seasons. We had dug deep and found that buried deep beneath this mess of a man was a monumental man. I remember the day like it was yesterday. We had just achieved a massive breakthrough. I couldn't wait to get home and share with Heather what we had uncovered. And then he said it.

"I think you need to go to this place called OnSite."

"OnSite? Is that a mountain one climbs to declare to the world he is finally healed? If so, I'm in!"

"Well, not really. It's a seven-day experiential-therapy retreat."

Insert screeching brake sounds here.

"Um, Al? Didn't I just hit a milestone? Haven't we uncovered stuff over the last two years that makes the torturous experience such as the one you just described needless? Why in the world would anyone go somewhere to have therapy for *seven straight days*?" I asked. Okay, so it was more like a plea.

Two years, twice a month, and sometimes more. And the man I've spilled my deepest, darkest secrets to tells me to go to rehab!

"It's not like rehab, Carlos. It's *experiential* therapy. Not *experimental* therapy. It's really cool. I've actually gone myself. I think it will be the push you need to get you over the hump."

I realized two very important things: (1) Two years of therapy had not gotten me over "the hump" after all, and (2) just seven days of *nonstop* therapy could.

I exhaled deeply, thanked Al, told him I'd look into it, and went on my way. Four weeks later I found myself in a minivan with my suitcase, my wife, and my three kids.

"Daddy? Where are we taking you again?" the middle child asked.

"It's called OnSite. It's a place where Daddy is going to go work on fixing some things inside him."

"Is it like church?"

"No, baby. It's not like church. It's not a Christian place. It's more like summer camp for grownups. I'll be staying in a cabin with roommates I don't know yet. I think I saw that there was a horseshoe pit in the brochure. And I heard I get to play with horses!"

The more I described this place out loud to my

nine-year-old, the more I wanted to tell Heather to turn the van around. What in the world was I thinking?

"Daddy," the nine-year-old said, "how are they going to fix you without Jesus?"

That question echoed in my head for at least fifteen seconds before I replied, "I don't know. I really don't know."

About fifteen minutes from OnSite, I realized I had not called my parents yet. This was a big deal only because I was going dark for the next seven days. One of the commitments you make when you go to this experience is that you relinquish any outside communication for the entirety of the program. So no phone calls, no email, no texts, no Twitter, no Netflix, no Netflix, no Netflix.

You actually have to *give* them your phones.

Lord come quickly. *Seven days.*

I grabbed my phone back from Losiah, my six-year-old, who was playing Candy Crush. I had the fleeting thought that maybe he was the one in need of therapy when he burst into tears for making him surrender my phone.

I called my parents.

The thing about calling my parents is that, inevitably, it becomes an event. One parent will always tell me not to say anything until the other parent is near the phone. Then they put me on speaker, which results in both parties having to repeat absolutely everything at least three times. It's hardly efficient, but it's us.

"Okay. So, where are you going again, *mijito*?" my mom asked.

"I'm going on a retreat, Mom. It's like a counseling retreat. For seven days."

By this point, the word *retreat* was mocking me. I wasn't

quite sure what else to call this, but I was pretty sure "communication prison" was not uplifting enough.

"Why are you going? Did you do something wrong? Is everything okay?"

"Mom. It's okay. We could *all* use some counseling every so often. Maybe not quite *this* much, but at least some." This is why I love my mother. She always believes the best in her son—as should all mothers.

"Everything is fine. Honestly though, I don't know why I'm going. I just know that I've gone my entire life receiving blessing after blessing, and then rubbing crap on it. Maybe I'm going there to stop ruining the good things in my life."

"I don't think you do that," she replied.

I love my mother.

And then, like a Morgan Freeman voice-over in some epic commercial, my dad spoke up.

"Can I tell you a story?"

"I have ten minutes. Can you make it quick?"

(I hope you read the following story in the voice of Morgan Freeman, because I swear my dad sounds like a Latino version of him.)

"When I was early in my ministry in Panama, I was preaching a three-day revival in a small church by the ocean. That first night I preached *mi corazon* out. I preached hard and loud. Many were touched by God. Toward the end of the invitation, Ms. Ramirez stood up in the second row. She made her way to the center aisle and walked very slowly toward the front. When she finally got to me, I asked Ms. Ramirez why she had come forward. Her answer was simple.

"'Pastor, I need you to pray that the Lord cleans the

cobwebs out of my life. I have so many cobwebs. Could you please pray?' she asked me.

"And so I obliged. I prayed that the Lord would clean the cobwebs out of her life. She thanked me and went on her way. On night two of the revival—"

I stopped him.

"I just got to the retreat place. I'm gonna have to let you go. I need to say bye to Heather and the kids."

"No, Son. You need to listen for another few minutes. Please."

I was a nervous wreck, and my dad's voice had always been soothing to me, so I said, "All right, but hurry."

He picked back up. "Night two of the revival, I saw her get up again—Ms. Ramirez. And she came walking down the aisle with a little more certainty.

"'Pastor, could you pray again? Could you please pray again that the Lord cleans the cobwebs out of my life?' she asked.

"I reminded her I had prayed the night before for this very thing, and that the Lord would honor our prayer. But she insisted I pray again. And so I did. *Our Father, Ms. Ramirez is obviously very concerned at the state of her life. Would you please help her clean up her life so she may honor you best with it? Please clean the cobwebs out of her life.*

"Son, listen to me. The last night of the revival—I couldn't believe it—she got up again. She made her way down the aisle even faster this night. I wondered if she was going to tell me that her life had begun to take a turn for the better—that the Lord had begun to clean the cobwebs.

"'Pastor Fermin, Pastor Fermin, please, one last time? Can you please pray that the Lord cleans the cobwebs—'

"I stopped her mid-sentence. I stopped her because I realized that we were praying the wrong prayer.

"And so I prayed, *Father, we do not ask you tonight to clean the cobwebs from Ms. Ramirez's life. In fact, Lord, keep them there for now. But tonight we ask for something much greater. Tonight we ask that you KILL THE SPIDER in Ms. Ramirez's life. In the name of Jesus I pray. Amen.*

"Carlos, I have watched you your entire life. You are a professional at cleaning the cobwebs from your life. You are amazing at playing the part and being used by God in spite of your circumstances. But do not go to this place and try to clean up your life. That won't work. You have to kill the spider. You must find the producer of all the cobwebs in your life and kill it. It is much more difficult, but *that* is why you are there. To *kill* the spider."

I don't remember much of the next few minutes. I mean, I remember hugging my family. I remember slowly making my way to the registration table. But the thought that took over everything else was that I had never heard my life explained more accurately than how my father had just summed it up.

I realized I was there to kill the spider. To kill the freaking spider. Now I just had to find it.

And, my friends, find it I did. I imagine one of these things is running through your head right now:

1. I don't think I have a problem with spiders, but how can I know for sure?
2. I think I have two hundred spiders, so how will I kill them all?
3. I know my spider; I just can't imagine killing it.

I can't promise you that this book will accomplish for you what seven straight days of therapy did for me. I hope this book is *nothing* like seven straight days of therapy.

But I can promise you this: This book will take you on a journey that should not be taken alone. So I'll share my story to give you hope in yours, and together we will face the spiders with the power of the God who makes the earth spin and float. Because with God, *all things* are possible.

What Is the Spider in Your Life?

You are probably wondering how in the world you are going to identify the spider in your life when you can't even get the cobwebs out of the way to see it. Well, let's begin with a couple of questions you can think about as we dig deeper.

- What sort of behaviors jumped out at the mention of "cleaning the cobwebs"?
- What sort of words come to mind at the phrase *kill the spider*. These don't have to be deep. We aren't searching to immediately define anything.
- What would *your* family say are things you need to work on? Hint: these are normally cobwebs.
- Growing up, what were the things you often got in trouble for?

COBWEBS

As I signed in for the retreat, I couldn't help but think about this charming metaphor my dad shared. There was definitely something profound there. I got it on a surface level, but I also knew there was more there that I needed to think about. Being at OnSite would allow me to really dive in.

Can we all agree that *nobody* likes to live in a house filled with spiders? Unless you have a pet spider—then you can skip this part.

Anyway, nobody—absolutely nobody—likes to walk into a cobweb. Remember the last time this happened to you? There was probably not a whole lot of grace involved in your reaction. You didn't walk into a cobweb, slowly stop, smile a crooked smile, reach into your pocket, and pull out a mirror. You didn't then pull out your hanky and slowly dab at your face, using your pocket mirror to methodically make your way around your face to pick off little bits of the cobweb.

No, this is not how you reacted to the cobweb.

Upon stumbling into said cobweb, you launched into what looked like a full-body seizure. Your arms flew up above your head, flailing frantically around. And as soon as you adequately swept your three-foot perimeter with your thrashing arms, you went for your face. You swiped at your face repeatedly. You also spat because, inevitably, some of the cobweb ended up in your piehole. This, my friends, is what happens when we stumble into cobwebs.

It's safe to assume that not one of us wants to live in an environment where we are running into these all the time. So we clear them out of the way, especially if they are in areas where we encounter them every day. Cobwebs in doorways, cobwebs in walkways, cobwebs under lamp shades—places we will be accessing daily and don't want them there.

But what if they are up in the corner of the room, tucked away in our bedroom closets or beneath the lip of a stair? If the cobwebs are in places where nobody is looking, we don't mind them so much. Who cares to clean the cobwebs in your basement, garage, or attic? No one. Why? Because they're not bothering us.

And when they stop bothering us, we forget about them . . . until the spider, which created that cobweb in the first place, comes crawling out.

Cobwebs are not welcomed, but we get used to them—and we get used to cleaning up after them. So what are some real-life cobwebs? I want to share how I began to recognize my personal cobwebs and give you some general tools for getting rid of the spiders that keep you repeating these behaviors. (I define a real-life cobweb as a medicator that brings false comfort to a lie.)

Body Image

Let's start with one of the mothers of all webs.

Back in 2012, I stepped on something that I had not stepped on in a *long* time. It wasn't a cockroach. It wasn't a LEGO left in my hallway as a booby trap by my five-year-old son that would take me down at 2:00 a.m. It was a scale. And that bad boy greeted me with this number: 225. I'm 5'9" and all of the websites were telling me that to be "healthy," I was supposed to be a whopping 175. Game over. I was fat and there was nothing that was gonna get me unfat because I have the follow-through of a dad on the sofa on a Sunday afternoon with leaves to rake. Earlier in my life, at about ten pounds heavier, I had a friend who would gently jab me for my weight. He'd call my neck "preacher neck" and poke my belly in the name of "fun." Hilarious, right? No, it stung. It stung every time. And every time I would try to lose the weight, it was always for *them*. It was always for what I looked like on the outside and for the world outside of me.

My weight loss always failed. The cobweb of attaining a certain appearance would not only not get cleaned; it grew and grew and grew. Unfortunately, at the time, I didn't realize that the only way to get rid of this cobweb was to either have a photoshop artist follow me around at every moment of my life, or to get healthy for the sake of health and not for the sake of body image. When God created man, God didn't create a body image to shoot for. That's our own doing. And if this is your main issue, if this is your main cobweb, well I can completely relate. When I killed the spider behind this web, I lost more than forty pounds. And I kept it off, because I stopped chasing the impossible. I began chasing God instead.

Gossip

I'm an average singer. But even with my average voice, singing opportunities kept coming for me all throughout my twenties and into my early thirties. I knew I wasn't an incredible singer, but that didn't keep me from leading worship in some of the largest churches and conferences in the country. That didn't keep me from signing a two-record deal with the biggest record label in Christian music. But the higher up I got in the industry, the more it would hurt to hear people talk about my "average" voice. There was one publication that ripped my first record apart. They may as well have ripped my soul apart. I went *off* on them on my blog. I went on a witch hunt and began to spit rumors in order to somehow feel as though I was better than they were. Once the comments began flooding onto my blog article titled "How Dare They!" I began to feel incredible. Such a rush. Like a drug. The cobweb was spinning out of control. I began a blog hunt against their magazine and its credibility. And every time I hit "publish," I took a hit from the cobweb called gossip.

One day the editor of the paper called. "Hey, man, I'm really sorry about how we covered your record. I know we used some language that was insulting and for that I'm sorry. But is there any way that you could stop with the witch hunt? It's hurting us. It's hurting me. What can I do to help?" It was like I stepped right into a *really cold* shower. Like the fog had been lifted and I was suddenly standing there. Completely aware of the damage I had inflicted. The cobweb of gossip was *all over* the home in my heart, and I needed to clean it soon.

"Man. I'm so sorry. I didn't think that my little corner of the web was gonna inflict any sort of pain on you guys. I'll delete all the articles. Thanks for apologizing."

It seemed like an easy fix. I deleted the blog posts, but all that did was clean the cobwebs. The spider was still there, whispering to me, "You only matter as much as other people tell you that you matter." Until I get over *that* particular lie, I will gossip *every single time* I'm wounded.

Artificial Intimacy

It doesn't take a behavioral therapist or a PhD in psychology to get to the bottom of our need for intimacy. We crave it, and we often settle for fake intimacy when we can't find a true connection with someone. We turn to our screens to fulfill this deep-seated desire for a fix. Sometimes that happens through our obsession with online interaction. We can allow ourselves to be absorbed by television shows where we become attached to the characters and almost live vicariously through their experience. At its worst, this need leads to deeper and darker cobwebs such as addiction to pornography or promiscuity.

Imagine you were at the grocery store and you had worn your best outfit that day and your hair and makeup were on point (unless you are bald and don't wear makeup like me). You were just minding your own business walking up and down the aisles and someone walked up to you and tapped you on the shoulder. You turned around to see the most beautiful human creation (next to your significant other, of course) smiling at you. "Can I just tell you. You have an amazing smile." And then, just as they appeared in your lane, they disappear. *Woah.* That felt *amazing.* I mean, I love my wife and you love your significant other, but that felt *good.* Maybe next week, if you wear the same outfit and show up at the same time in the same aisle, you can get that compliment again! This isn't some evil scheme. This is simply humanity. It feels amazing to be noticed.

Now let's just replace this impossible interaction with a more relatable one. The one that happens on our screens. The feeling that rushes inside of you when you get that intimacy from strangers is amazing. But we have to remember: it's not real. If we aren't careful, we can let these cobwebs take over. And before we know it we will be tangled up in artificial intimacy and not know what is real and what is not.

It's starting out with healthy desire. A healthy desire to be seen. Cobwebs don't have to start off in these nasty dark corners of our souls. No, they can start from places of innocence and purity. So even if you aren't immediately finding these massive webs in your life, look in the safe spaces. They are there. We all have them.

Alcohol

Alcohol won't be a cobweb for everyone, but you know if it is for you. Maybe you can't stop at having one beer after work because it turns into four. By the time you get done with the third you feel nice and numb, and you think, *This feels so much better than the reality of my life.* So you keep going back to that place of numbness. The numbness is medicating the problems that you have in many areas of your life that need correction. But that is gonna take work—a lot more work than the numbness takes. The problem with this cobweb isn't just that it keeps coming back, but that it gets bigger and bigger each time. I'm not saying alcohol is always a cobweb. I love having a glass of Blanton's Kentucky Bourbon when I'm with friends. It *is* a cobweb when that occasional drink with friends becomes one of those messy parts of everyday life.

Take, for instance, a time when Heather and I had not been connecting. Nothing crazy, just not connecting for a few days. What we really needed was some time together dreaming. That is what always does it for us. But instead of connecting, we did something else that we both find enjoyable. We invited a few friends over for dinner and drinks. After two glasses of wine I suddenly stopped feeling the deep pit in my gut about where we were as a couple. It felt strangely gone. And so, you know what I wanted? For it to be completely gone. So I drank another glass. And maybe another. My marriage woes felt light-years away. But they weren't. They were staring me right in the face. But that is when drinking for me becomes a cobweb: when it covers truth.

Social Media Addiction / Approval Addiction

Social media can become a cobweb in two ways. You are either getting your self-confidence needs met by being validated by the "Likes" from some stranger or friend as we talked about in the last section on artificial intimacy, *or* you are desperately addicted to wishing your life looked like someone else's. This is where Carlos Whittaker's trouble began with this particular cobweb. Instagram is supposed to be the place where we share our lives with our friends. What it quickly turned into for me is the place where I go to wish my life looked like someone else's. It sneaks up on you. One day you are enjoying your life, the next day you are wishing your life looks like someone else's. And it really began to affect me when Snapchat showed up. It became my FOMO Headquarters. What is FOMO you may be asking? FOMO means the Fear Of Missing Out. I'll never forget the first time social media gave me this feeling. It was right around the time I went to OnSite. A bunch of my friends got invited on a trip without me; the group of friends whom I *always* got invited to go with. It was pure torture watching their snaps and their Instagram posts of all the fun they were having. I was spinning some massive conspiracy theories as to how and when they decided that I was no longer part of their club. Maybe it was because I hadn't hit the level of success I was supposed to? Maybe it was because I hadn't sent them a Christmas card that year? Maybe it was because I wasn't as smart as they were? Maybe it was because *I am no longer worthy of friends? OMG; why why why?*

You know the feeling. It's not simply seeing someone you have never met and wishing you had their life. It sneaks up on you in your real friendships. I was tempted to live my life in a way that would impress those who were impressing me and end up being the most inauthentic version of myself in the history of myself.

This web. There is no way of cleaning this cobweb

without it being spun moments later in another corner. You know what you will be tempted to do to get rid of this particular cobweb once and for all? You will just delete the social media apps off of your phone. But guess what? The spider is still there, lurking in the corner, waiting to spin the web without your social media apps.

We were made in the image of God, not in the image of [insert your "instajealousy" here]. The cobweb is spun when you are going to social media for the validation only God Himself should provide.

Cobweb Cleaning

These are just four examples of cobwebs—only four. You may recognize yourself in the ones I described or they may prompt you to identify others.

Now, let's see if I can describe how the cleaning normally goes down. Most likely, the first thing that happens is avoidance. We avoid them until they show up in our face, right? We see them in the corners of our souls but don't really do anything until somebody else points them out for us.

And then, just as I noted earlier, we go into a panic, flailing our arms and swatting at our faces, trying to remove the cobweb. We clean up the initial nastiness of the cobweb by offering an apology to the person we have hurt with our gossip or by promising our spouse that we will stop drinking so much after work. Now we feel clean.

Maybe we do a little follow-up cleaning to make sure we got it all. We download a sermon or inspirational message that speaks to our issue and really motivates us to stay on the straight and narrow. Maybe we hear a quote that offers a great takeaway or nugget of wisdom and we write it on a Post-It note to stick on the mirror to remind us every day. And maybe if we read it enough times we will not be tempted to repeat our offending behavior. Maybe we can conquer our issue. We might even go all in and get it tattooed somewhere to make it permanent. But we all know how it goes. Eventually, we get so used to seeing what's in front of our faces every day that we forget it's there. We overlook it and the significance fades. And *poof*, we're back to ignoring the cobwebs.

It's not enough to identify the cobwebs and work on them. Our strength will never be enough. When we rely on ourselves alone, we end up swatting at the same cobwebs over and over. Paul says, "And He has said to me, 'My grace is sufficient for you, for power is perfected in weakness.' Most gladly, therefore, I will rather boast about my weaknesses, so that the power of Christ may dwell in me" (2 Corinthians 12:9 NASB).

Is Paul telling us that by simply boasting about his weakness, the power of Christ began to dwell in him? He really expects us to believe that? Well, yes, he does.

And, yes, *it* does. Our two primary weapons in this spider-killing battle are exactly what most Christians forget we need.

We will never kill our spiders with podcasts, seminars, conferences, conversations, leadership principles, devotional apps, Scripture tattoos, or killer Instagram images with motivational quotes on them. They are great and work for a moment—literally, one moment. But that stuff isn't and wasn't created to address the deeper needs. It won't completely and totally change you from the inside out.

No, the sort of transformation Paul was talking about only comes from two tools: the Word of God and prayer. That is all.

You can sugarcoat it all you want. You can say this answer is too elementary and that your addictions, affairs, and afflictions need all of those other things as well. But the truth is the weapons we have been handed are found inside the Word of God and our walking and talking with Him. Yes, there are intricacies we will dance with, but for now, I want you to know that if you have been trying for years to defeat your spider with tools that develop your own strength, you weren't built to be strong enough. You won't ever be strong enough.

We can't and won't ever be able to live this Christian life in and with our own strength. We must quit attempting to clean the cobwebs every day. We must quit trying to live perfect Christian lives. Stop trying. Allow Christ to live your messy Christian life for you. You will only discover how to pull that off in the Word of God, so let's put down our little cobweb-cleaning brooms and grab our spider-destroying weapons.

What Are the Cobwebs in Your Life?

I listed four common cobwebs. Maybe those aren't the ones that keep popping up for you. Maybe you find yourself repeatedly dealing with anger or fear of intimacy or some other relationship struggle. Cobwebs aren't necessarily major moral failings or criminal activity, just something that keeps you in turmoil and distanced from God. As we move forward, spend some time trying to identify what your cobwebs are so that you have some idea of where you need to start.

Ask yourself:

- What habits do I keep struggling to break? (Hint: A good place to look for clues is your annual New Year's resolution list. What makes the list over and over?)
- What area of my life seems to stay in turmoil? Where do I feel I'm constantly failing?

THE CIRCLE AT ONSITE

I hugged Heather and my kids good-bye. The kids were overflowing with excitement seeing where Dad was going to spend the week. It was the most epic-looking farm ever—horses galloping in the distance, a three-story farmhouse with a wraparound porch straight out of *Gone With the Wind*, and three dogs with floppy ears that gathered at our feet, greeting us with licks.

Hugging the wife brought a sense that this seven-day journey was it. The summit was near. I was close to that breakthrough we'd been expecting and needing. I knew that if I focused and climbed, I would get there. But there was also a storm on the horizon. We had been in crisis mode for so long, and our relationship, our life together, and our future was still fragile; if I didn't do this right, all the prayer in the world wouldn't save me from dying on the side of our marriage mountain. I needed to climb. And I needed to do it now.

After my family drove away, I walked into the main room where a smiling lady greeted me with a bag filled with goodies. I was escorted to the cabin where I would be rooming with two other participants in the Living Centered Program.

The Living Centered Program is designed to help you get back to the center of who you are. I didn't know what all of that was supposed to mean at the time, but if I knew anything in that moment, it was that I was in no way centered.

As I walked in and began to explore the "cabin"—a term that really sells the place short because it was gorgeous—I saw bags on two of the three queen-sized beds in the room and poked around a bit to see if there was anything on the surface that would give me a clue about my roomies.

One of the beds had a Bible on it. The other bed had a *Lowrider Truck* magazine and a bag that smelled of weed. That told me a lot about them. I dropped my bags on my bed and headed to orientation.

There was a nervous energy in the room from the forty strangers trying to figure each other out. The second I walked in I was annoyed by seven of them. They were the loud ones, and I was pretty sure I could guess what their spiders were. I texted Heather: "This. Is. Going. To. SUCK."

There was a sign above the main doors that read, "Trust the process. Celebrate the miracles." Okay, sign. Deal. But for the love of everything holy, please deliver me some miracles.

"Welcome to OnSite!" boomed a deep voice that had the strength of the man that plays Santa in the local Christmas pageant and the gentleness of Mr. Rogers. "Go ahead and have a seat," he said. All forty participants took a seat in a massive circle as the man introduced himself. "Good evening, friends. My name is Bill, and I'm the clinical director here. Listen, I know this sounds crazy, but by this time next week, these forty people, who you don't know, will become some of the dearest friends you have ever made, and you won't be able to imagine your life without them."

Okay, Bill. That's cute. But can I go home now?

The first thing we did was go around the circle to introduce ourselves and explain why we were there, or why we thought we were there. There were only two rules: for the entire week we were not allowed to say our last name, and we were not allowed to say what we did for a living. I found this fascinating and immediately began to try to figure out what everyone did.

As people went around the circle, my pastoral heart could not help but feel that I could help these people. They simply needed what I have. They were so sad. Maybe I was there to help them! When my turn came up I told everyone the story my dad had told me just before I arrived—that I was there to kill the spider. I have to confess, I didn't give my dad credit, so everyone immediately thought I was a philosopher.

At the end of the kumbaya circle, Bill said, "Now I'm going to introduce you guys to your therapists for the week. You will be divided into four groups of ten. You will be spending a large part of every day with that group. This will not be one-on-one therapy. All the therapy will happen in the confines of a small group."

The first therapist looked like a shorter version of Cameron Diaz. She was supernice and bubbly as she called the names of her ten. I was not one. The next therapist looked to be straight out of Woodstock. She had the most epic silver hair in a braid that reached down to the back of her legs. When she spoke, it was filled with depth and peace. I threw up a quick prayer that she would be my therapist.

Nope.

Next was a woman who was probably the oldest in the room. She was seventy or so with bright red hair and rings on every finger. Her name was Nancy and she looked exactly like how I imagine a gypsy fortune-teller would look. And when Nancy opened her mouth, it was not a peaceful tone. It was a bossy, kind of know-it-all tone. *Please, God, not her. I don't want to be in her group.* Seven names into her group of ten, mine had not been called, but the seven people I picked out in the room that annoyed me were. And then . . . I was number eight. *Thanks, God. I really appreciate Your looking out for me on this. This is never gonna work*, I thought, shaking my head.

I have to admit God must have a wicked sense of humor to drop me in a group with all the people I really didn't want to spend time with. Can you imagine? Have you ever been in a situation where you were forced to deal with someone you didn't get along with and saw no way out?

Maybe it's a coworker in your office who makes your life difficult by not carrying their own weight. It could be a person at church who tries to run everything and forces their opinion on everyone else. You might have that friend who is always a train wreck and brings their drama into everyone else's life, asks for advice even though they never take it, and makes everyone around them miserable.

We all have those people around us. Heck, we might even BE that person in our circle. They keep us distracted from figuring out what we need to be fixing in ourselves.

They either keep us so busy helping them sort out their issues that we neglect our own, or we are fooled into thinking that, by comparison, we aren't all that bad, so maybe we don't need to do any more work.

I was beginning to think that either I would grow a ton by learning how to deal with difficult people (Can you say, "false-piety cobweb"?), or I wouldn't make any progress being stuck with them (the self-pity cobweb).

Bill announced: "You guys have thirty more minutes with your phones. Then we are going to take them until the end of the week. You will survive. I promise."

So I called Heather from my room and told her I felt God had sent me there because I really might be able to help some of those people. She immediately responded, "You are not there to fix them. You are there to fix you."

Why does she always do this? She is the most gentle spiritual sage you will ever meet. Her comment took me sprinting down a memory lane that I had not run down before. How many times had I done this? How many times had I ignored the plank in my eye for the plank in another's eye? Not in a sinful or negative way. It was always in the name of ministry. For more than fifteen years as I was on staff at churches, this was the conundrum I found myself in. I spent years helping other people while ignoring the glaring symptoms of unhealth in my own life. If you are in any way involved in ministry this is a vital moment for you. Sometimes you have to *completely* stop helping others in order to help yourself. It was time to get selfish in a way I had not been selfish before. And I needed to know that it was okay. This was the first of many hard facts I had to face as I started on this journey. They asked us to trust the process, and I thought I was ready to do that, but I was seriously questioning how it could possibly work when I was stuck with people I knew were going to make the process difficult.

The truth is, Heather was right, although I had no clue what needed fixing. Remember, I thought I'd had the breakthrough a few weeks earlier in therapy. What was this spider? How in the world could I find, chase, and kill this freaking forty-year-old spider in only seven days? Little did I know that my spider was doing push-ups in the corner of my soul, getting ready to fight for its life while I fought for mine.

Have You Identified the Spider Yet?

As you dig through the messy parts of your life to locate the spider so you can get rid of it, you are going to start coming across some really tough stuff. You have to be prepared to look at yourself honestly and be open to learning some unflattering things about yourself. Coming to terms with that is the hard part. Once you accept the fact that you have work to do, it's a whole lot easier to buckle down and start doing it. Are you ready to get to work, or are you still trying to pretend that what's wrong isn't big enough to need this kind of attention?

- Do you allow distractions or comparisons to keep you from identifying your spider?
- Have you identified something you think might be a spider that keeps creating cobwebs in your life? Are you ready to track it down and rid yourself of it for good?

C
H
A
P
T
E
R

4

✳

THE SEVEN-YEAR-
OLD MAGICIAN

One of the first things that I noticed in our gatherings
at OnSite was that Bill and Nancy kept talking about
our "young selves." The five-year-old me. The seven-year-
old me. And God bless them, but I had a pretty fantastic
childhood. It was the twenty-five-year-old me that was
wounded and needed therapy. Surely it wasn't this young
version of me. I grew up in the burbs with Christian parents who loved me and signed me up for soccer and always
came to my games. I was never without anything. I always
felt loved and supported. Every single time we would start
to talk about the "young" us, I was annoyed. I could see in
my friends at OnSite that they had some jacked-up stuff
happening in their childhood, and for that I felt like they
needed this part of the experience more than I did.

"I'm glad you have such a fond memory of your childhood, Carlos," Nancy encouraged me the first morning. I
had just gotten done telling her my problem with the whole

"young Carlos" experiential therapy treatment. It wasn't gonna work. My childhood made Ricky Schroder on Silver Spoons jealous.

"I get it. But just because you had an incredible childhood, just because your memories serve you a sitcom of adolescence, doesn't mean there isn't some work to be done." Nancy sat me down and, like a modern-day Yoda, took me on a journey toward seven years old. She started me out at one of my main issues. The belief that I am faking it through this life. This common theme that somehow I have convinced everyone in my life that I am something better than I really am. That I have fooled my way into this position in life. All it took was one question from her to cause me to rush into a moment that I had long since forgotten. A moment from seven-year-old Carlos that would be a pivot point in my story.

"When did you start believing you were a fraud? Was it something you said or did as a child? Take a minute and really think about it."

It didn't take a minute. It came rushing back to me like a roaring river. I *was* seven. And I was at church.

In the '90s there was a group called the Power Team. They performed at almost every large youth event I was a part of, where they gave demonstrations of their God-given strength. They would break cinder blocks with their foreheads, place each other in handcuffs and rip them apart, or blow up hot water bottles with their lungs until the hot water bottle exploded, all while sprinkling Scripture throughout, convincing us that somehow God was giving them this strength in the moment.

And maybe He was. All I knew was that I went home

from every Power Team show and would attempt some feat of strength they showed us. One time, I grabbed a phone book in my thirteen-year-old hands and began to pray that God would somehow give me the strength to rip it in half. I really thought I could do it because only a few hours before, as one of the Power Team was attempting to rip the phone book in half, another member was screaming into the microphone for us to *"Pray harder!!! Pray harder that God gives him the strength!!!"*

So I would pray harder in the stands, and lo and behold, the brother would rip that thing in half. And every single student in that gymnasium would go absolutely crazy.

But no matter how hard I prayed at home, God never gave me the strength to rip that phone book in half.

The church I was a part of in the '80s was heaven to me. I remember absolutely zero spiritual abuse or malice like you hear about from so many my age—just a group of loving people who gathered three or four nights a week for church stuff. It was a place filled with friends and songs and laughter and every so often something horrible like handbell choir.

We had two Sunday morning services and one evening service. Many times the evening services were replaced with some sort of event or concert. Sunday nights were some of my favorite memories—musicals, concerts, sing-alongs, movies.

I'll never forget this one evening in particular when I was seven. It is burned in my memory for a few reasons, one of them being that the next day I was going to Adam Shaver's birthday party.

That morning in church, Pastor Harris announced that

the evening service would be a magic show. *A magic show?* I was all in. I begged my mom and dad to let me come back that night. They didn't think twice.

I found myself sitting in the front row on the left side of the balcony that night. It was the best seat at Briarlake Baptist Church. I could see everything. There were tables all over the stage draped in black cloth covering whatever wonders were beneath them. The magic man was ready.

It seemed like an eternity before the magic man appeared on stage to start the show. I don't remember one single trick he performed, but I do remember the feeling of total and complete awe. I remember lots of applause and lots of laughing and oohs and aahs. But more than anything, I remember sitting next to my mom when the magic man asked if anyone wanted to come forward. *Come forward? To hang with magic man? To learn a trick? Is this a joke? Of course I want to go down.* I saw a stream of people walking down the aisles. If I didn't act fast, I would lose my shot to hang with this guy, so I tugged on my mom's pants. She looked at me like, "Really? You want to go down there?" *Yes, Mom. I want to go down there, and if we don't move now, I won't get to meet this magic man and learn his tricks.* I didn't say that, but I thought it. Had I said that out loud, things might have gone differently. She looked so overjoyed. "Go," she said. And with that, I was off. I leapt out of my seat and ran down the stairs of the balcony. I sprinted around the corner of the lobby and back into the sanctuary. There was a crowd gathering at the stage, but I was small enough to wiggle my way to the front. I couldn't find Mr. Magic Man anywhere. Then I saw him on the left side of the stage. He had his hand on a man's shoulder and was talking to him. There were lots of people crying. *Why are all these people crying?*

That's when I felt a hand on my shoulder. It was Ms. Platt. She was the church pianist. She had a smile as big as the Texas sky spread across her face. "I'm so proud of you, Carlos. Why don't you come with me?"

Proud of me? Go with her? Where? What in the world is she proud of? What's going on?

I followed Ms. Platt to one of the pews in the front row, and she told me to close my eyes and repeat after her.

Okay.

So I repeated a prayer something like this:

"Dear Jesus, I invite You into my heart. Thank You for forgiving me of my sins. Thank You for dying on the cross for me. Amen."

What is going on?

She was overjoyed and led me to a back room where my mom was waiting. My mom hugged me so long and hard that I knew in that moment I had messed up. Big time. Even at seven years old, I realized that these people were convinced I had done something I had not actually done. Everyone was so happy for me.

Everyone except me, because I knew the truth. I had gone to the front to learn a magic trick, and I had performed the biggest trick of them all. I had convinced a room full of people that I wanted to become a Christian. And I did want that, but not right then. Everyone was telling me that I was a Christian, and I knew I was not. Everyone was so excited, and I was so terrified.

What did I just do?

The next day my parents took me back to church. I

remember walking into the office part of the church that had big oak doors and really fancy carpet.

"You get to meet with Pastor Harris today, Carlos," my mom told me.

What? No. Please, God, no. It was hard enough to keep up the charade around my mom and dad and Sunday school teacher. But now I was gonna have to lie to the pastor?

"Good afternoon, Carlos."

Wow. There he was. Pastor Harris. He was even kinder and more mythical looking than I imagined. I remember him asking me a few questions. These were questions filled with Bible verses mixed with common sense. And I realized something at seven years old. This was my way out. This was the place I felt safe enough to get out of this lie.

I kept yelling at myself, *Just tell him the truth! Just tell him you went down the aisle to learn a magic trick! Just tell him the truth.*

But I didn't. And he handed me a Bible with my name engraved on the front. And with that Bible under my arm and a lump in my throat, I walked out of Pastor Harris's study and into the biggest lie of my life.

There I was, swept up in the massive emotions of everyone around me, and in order to please the people who were so proud of me, I kept playing the part. I kept acting in this story I stumbled into.

You see, the stories we find ourselves pushed into are not always stories with sinister roots. All too often, we say yes to a relationship with no clue that it will take us down a road of embarrassment and gut-wrenching pain that we couldn't possibly foresee. But nobody can know about the mistake we made, so we don't tell anyone and keep up the façade. One lie leads to another, and then we find ourselves trapped in good intentions. We are scared of everyone else getting hurt, so we stay in the story.

You don't have to be seven years old and confused. You can be fifty-seven years old and confused. What starts off as good intentions can turn quickly into cobwebs that trap you for years. Little did I know that the simple, untold truths I found myself spinning those few days at church would ultimately lead to more spiritual pain in my life than I knew was possible.

How many of our good intentions end up turning into the biggest cobwebs ever?

How many times have you had right reasons in mind that ended up destroying you?

It's not enough just to have good intentions. It's not enough to have strong conviction. When things begin to unravel—when cobwebs show up—you have a shot to stop it early. You have an opportunity to get to the root before it becomes life-consuming.

It's really true of all spiders. They don't start off that strong. They don't start off with that much reach. But the more we ignore them, the longer we allow them to feed on our mistakes and fears and spin their cobwebs of sin. Then it becomes so much harder to kill them.

Although the next few years of my church life were still some of the fondest memories I have of church, when someone would ask me if I was a Christian, I would suddenly freeze. And I would lie. I soon realized that with this lie, I was treated differently. People were proud of me. People were telling me how incredible I was. And it felt good.

At a young age, I was becoming a master of lies. It

then became easier not only to lie about being a Christian, but about all sorts of things—especially the things I could say to make someone think I was better than I really was. One lie after another. It became a part of who I was. I had become a liar. I was a liar. I believed this with all my heart. And if I had lied about the greatest thing I could ever lie about, well, every lie from that point on was a lesser evil.

Church services were especially brutal. Every time the pastor came to the end of his message, he would ask for people to pray in their hearts to receive Jesus, and I would pray all over again, hoping that one of those prayers would work. I hoped that one of those prayers would change the years of deceit I had spun around my faith. From my grownup perspective, I know I was absolutely following Jesus. I was a child of God living in His goodness, but somehow I was still racked by guilt. I felt like a fraud. It was exhausting.

Ask yourself these simple questions: What spiders are being given birth in my life, and what cobwebs are they spinning? What lies about myself am I turning into truths?

Is it the incredible feeling you got when you walked past that coworker and you felt them looking at you a little longer than your married self has experienced in a long time?

Spider born.

Maybe you walk past their desk an extra three times to keep that feeling alive.

Cobweb spun.

Could it be the little voice in your head that compares your social media following to others and tells you that you will never be successful or popular?

Spider born.

Maybe you end up spending a hundred dollars to buy

a thousand fake followers on Instagram to give yourself a boost.

Cobweb spun.

Are you telling yourself after two beers that this light and free sensation is how you are supposed to feel?

Spider born.

Maybe you end up going for the fourth and fifth beer every night to numb you to whatever pain you are feeling.

Cobweb spun.

Spiders can start small. But the good news is that when they are small, all it takes is keeping your gaze on God to kill them.

You know what you need to do. You need to trust the process God has laid in front of you. Go to God and acknowledge your sin. Give it to Him, and let Him be the strength in you to defeat the baby spiders.

Are You Ready to Search It Out?

Dealing with spiders is not fun, but if you go after the small spiders in your life as they come up, they don't have the opportunity to get big and strong. That makes them much easier to exterminate. To be clear: a spider is an agreement with a lie you believe. A cobweb is any medicator that brings false comfort to that lie. List them out, and deal with them here and now.

- Do you recognize a small spider that has recently started spinning cobwebs in your life?
- Where did it originate and what can you do to eradicate its influence?

I BELONGED TO THE CRAZIES

I woke up with a lump in my throat—actually, *lump* is putting the mountain in my esophagus lightly. There I was. Lying in a double bed seven feet from one stranger and fifteen feet from another. I wondered if they were awake and staring at the ceiling as well. At least I was within shouting distance of my family if these two roomies were more unstable than I currently was. My roommates were from Texas and California. There we were, together in our separate issues.

My bed was against the wall next to the door leading out of our room and into the Narnia of therapeutic retreat centers. It was the dark corner of the room. The bed on the opposite side was next to a massive window and the sun was pouring into the bedroom. I peeked to my left and saw both roommates still sound asleep. I leaned over in my bed to check my phone for Twitter updates and text messages I may have missed in the night. Oops. No phone.

I got up and prepared myself for this new normal. My ritual for the week went like this:

Wake up around 7:00 a.m.

Breakfast 7:30–8:00 a.m.

Large-Group Meditation Time 8–9:00 a.m.

Large-Group Class 9:15–11:00 a.m.

Small-Group Experiential Therapy 11–12:30 p.m.

Lunch 12:30–1:15 p.m.

Small Group 2–5:00 p.m.

Dinner 5:30–6:30 p.m.

Large-Group Activity 7–9:00 p.m.

Sleep

Repeat

I may not have been clear on this point, but this was like going through seven years of therapy in seven days. Yeah. Now you get it. The morning large-group times were almost like classroom experiences. We sat through a lecture from Bill, and then we had some class participation. We mostly went over the major medicators in our lives. What the program called medicators, I call cobwebs: alcohol, relational addictions, pornography, drugs, codependency, and so on. We would deal with one each day, and although I could not identify with many of the cobwebs my friends at OnSite were dealing with, what I learned was that webs cover up the real problem.

Our small-group gatherings were where the real work took place. These rooms contained the secrets and stuff that blockbuster movies are made of. The ten people in my group would become, over the forty-plus collective hours we would spend in that room together, some of my closest confidants—the safe ones. And it was in that safety, that I caught my first glimpse of healing.

You see, Bill repeatedly told us that thirty percent of the work would be done by working things out through our own story, and the other seventy percent of the work would be done by helping other people work out their story. Sounds a little like helping a friend move, right? Like, I'm going to pack you up and move you into a new house, get sweaty, and have a sore back, but it's not even my new house? Turns out that helping somebody else work through their story helps you work through yours. I didn't understand how that might be true until I became the Bad Dad for an hour.

"Who wants to go first?" Nancy asked.

Not a single person raised their hand.

Nancy wanted us to set up a life-size, three-dimensional picture of our families. But there was a catch: our family portrait needed to be our family when we were five years old. And we would need to pick other members of our group to portray not only us at five, but the nuclear family we had at five.

Over the course of the next few days I would play various roles in various people's stories. By the end of the week I was hoping to be nominated for a Tony Award.

Let's take Sharon's story. (Sharon and her story have been fabricated by me to show the premise of our therapy time and to paint a picture of what incredible work was done in our small group rooms. Sharon is not a real person.)

"Sharon" had been up-front with us all that she had not cried in over twenty years. Not because she didn't love or hurt, but because she simply didn't cry.

She picked someone in our group to be her at five. She placed her in the corner of the room by the door, and posed her in a position where she was almost walking out of the room.

And then she picked me to be her grandpa.

Immediately I thought to myself, *grandpa*? I'm officially over forty.

"Carlos, stand up," she ordered.

She stood me in the other corner of the room facing the five-year-old version of herself. She had me leaning toward her, almost wanting to chase her.

Then she chose someone to play her sister. She placed her sister sitting on a chair with her back facing both Sharon and her grandpa.

Sharon stepped back from the tableau she created and said, "Yup. Perfect. This was us."

What in the world?

Nancy chimed in.

"Sharon, talk to us. What are we looking at?"

Sharon went into a story about her childhood that absolutely wrecked me. She got so deep so fast. But she was still emotionless. I had *way* more emotion at the story she was telling than she did.

As she was telling us what was going on in her life, Nancy, the director in this experiential and therapeutic play, was helping move Sharon from thought to thought with the precision of a brain surgeon. I was mesmerized by both the story that I was currently a part of and the pace at which Nancy was helping Sharon get to the root of the story.

The closer that Sharon got to the root of her issues, the more intently she began to stare into my eyes. But I had to remember: these were not the eyes of Carlos Whittaker that she was staring into. No. My eyes belonged to her grandpa, with whom she was about to have a moment that none of us were expecting.

It took about ten minutes of "pretend" conversation with Sharon's sister and grandpa to get us to that moment.

We were told not to break character at any time, so I just kept staring at Sharon.

"How do you feel about your grandpa, Sharon?" Nancy asked.

"I hate him. I hate him," Sharon responded very calmly.

"Why don't you tell your grandpa that?" Nancy prodded, pointing at me.

So Sharon turned to me and very calmly said, "I hate you. But you know I hate you. I've told you I hate you every time I have seen you the past twenty years. Look at what you did to my family. And look at what you have done to me!"

I wanted to yell back at Sharon that I, in fact, do love her, and she is worth so much more than she feels. But of course, that is what Carlos feels. Not her grandpa.

So I kept my trap shut.

Nancy continued pushing. "Sharon, are you feeling anything at all? Any anger? Any sadness?"

"Nope. Nothing."

And then Nancy did something that completely changed the way I saw her. She went from simply being a therapist to being an artist.

"Sharon, obviously you feel something. I mean, he messed with your head. Look at your sister, for God's sake. She is a wreck."

"Nope. Nothing."

We all watched Nancy go over to the corner of the room and bring back a large rubber block. It was about three feet tall by two feet wide. With it, she brought a rubber bat. She placed the bat in Sharon's hands and the block at her feet.

"Sharon, please tell your grandpa what he did to you and your family and how it makes you feel. Only, this time, I want you to simply tap the block with the bat. Slowly. Just tap it while talking to him."

Sharon stared directly into my eyes and began to speak.

Tap . . . tap . . . tap . . .

"Grandpa . . . You know I hate you."

. . . tap . . . tap . . .

"Remember all the times,"

. . . tap . . . tap . . .

"you would be the life of the party,"

. . . tap . . . tap . . .

"until your fourth drink in."

. . . tap . . .

"All my friends thought you were the man, Grandpa,"

. . . tap . . .

"and you were. You would be able to maintain your cool until about the fourth drink, Grandpa."

. . . tap . . . tap . . . tap . . .

"And then you would flip,"

. . . tap . . . tap . . .

"and nobody could tell us what was coming, Grandpa."

. . . TAP . . . TAP . . .

. . . TAP . . . TAP . . .

. . . TAP . . . TAP . . . TAP . . .

. . . TAP . . . TAP . . . TAP . . .

The taps turned from taps into thumps. As Sharon's voice increased in volume, so did the intensity of the bat hitting the block.

Nancy chimed in again, "Let him know how you feel, Sharon."

With the cadence of someone knocking at your front door, she screamed the next nine words while slamming that bat onto the block.

"I *hate* you for what you did to us!"

Yelling turned into screaming, and before you knew it, a single tear emerged at the corner of Sharon's left eye.

"Don't you smile at me, Grandpa! Do you hear me? I hate you! I *hate* you!"

I wasn't smiling. I was actually trying not to cry.

And with those last three words, Sharon actually broke the bat and fell onto the floor weeping uncontrollably. Weeping tears that had been trapped inside her for twenty years. I immediately left my position to go pick her up.

"Ah, ah, ah. Nope. Get back to your spot, Carlos," Nancy snapped.

Nancy walked over to Sharon and whispered something into her ears. Sharon stood up and looked at me.

"This pain you caused me can't hurt me anymore, Grandpa. It's over. I'm in charge of it. Not you."

"Carlos," Nancy said, "repeat after me, and say this while looking into Sharon's eyes: Sharon. My name is Carlos, and I am not your grandpa."

I said that to Sharon, and she had to say back to me: "Hi, Carlos. You are not my grandpa."

Nancy had us do this because there is such energy and emotion wrapped into our role-playing sessions that if you do not "de-role" it's possible for resentment to remain between the role-playing parties.

I'm grateful for that because Lord knows I didn't want Sharon to stick a knife in my back while I was sleeping.

I went to bed that night a little overwhelmed—overwhelmed

by the emotion of that first day, but also overwhelmed that Sharon knew why she was there. She knew the exact reason. And I was clueless.

My dad didn't abuse me. My mother loved me. What in the world was I going to do when it was my turn? Why had I made such poor decisions in life? Why was I rubbing crap all over my blessings time and time again?

I didn't know that first night, but I was about to find out.

Let's pause for a moment. I want to be clear about something: not everyone reading this book is going to need to go to an experiential therapy retreat deep in the woods of Tennessee in order to find and kill their spider.

But we all will have to dig. We are going to have to dig back to the point of trauma or the point of pain and stare it in the eyes. And we all aren't going to have Nancy and her flowing feather earrings with turquoise stones to guide us. The good news is we have a way better guide.

Nancy was invaluable to us in that tiny room where we spent the week, but God the Father is with us in this massive room we call life.

> Finally, be strong in the Lord and in the strength of his might. Put on the whole armor of God, that you may be able to stand against the schemes of the devil. For we do not wrestle against flesh and blood, but against the rulers, against the authorities, against the cosmic powers over this present darkness, against the spiritual forces of evil in the heavenly places. Therefore take up the whole armor of God, that you may be able to withstand in the evil day, and having done all, to stand firm. Stand

therefore, having fastened on the belt of truth, and having put on the breastplate of righteousness, and, as shoes for your feet, having put on the readiness given by the gospel of peace. In all circumstances take up the shield of faith, with which you can extinguish all the flaming darts of the evil one; and take the helmet of salvation, and the sword of the Spirit, which is the word of God, praying at all times in the Spirit, with all prayer and supplication.

EPHESIANS 6:10–18 ESV

This Scripture used to overwhelm me. I think because it was used in such a macho way when I was growing up. All Christian illustrators would draw these He-Man-looking characters with their epic weapons. Massive bulging muscles wielding their weapons of the faith. I would always think, *This is so not me. I am such a fairy Christian. I can barely push my lawn mower, much less carry all of that around.*

But as I approached my spider, the weapons that have been given to me in Scripture seem so much more ninja-like than he-man-like. And the most important weapon to get to the bottom of the "Where in the world is my spider?" question is the belt of truth.

Nancy was setting all of us up in that room to put on the belt of truth.

John 8:32 tells us that the "truth will set you free."

It's so true! Think about it for a second. Where does a police officer keep his gun, walkie-talkie, handcuffs, maybe a Taser? On the belt. If the officer has no belt, he has to hold all the weapons with his bare hands, and that's not gonna work. He suddenly loses eighty percent of his efficiency. (I totally just made up that percentage. Don't look it up.) But you get it. The belt of truth gives you *freedom* to use the remaining weapons.

So. Let's put it on.

What is your truth? Where did it go sideways?

Get back to that place—to the truth. We are going to need that belt of truth before we can get anywhere else. We don't want our pants falling down when the spider comes out to fight.

Sharon cried a lot that week. She cried when we passed a butterfly on a bush. She cried when she saw the sunset. She cried when we said good-bye. In every one of her tears I could see the reflection of something—peace and the beginning of true healing.

Who Might Be Part of Your Journey That You're Overlooking?

Being in Sharon's family portrait and taking on the role of her grandpa was an unbelievably uncomfortable experience for me, but it really brought home the realization that we aren't making this journey toward healing alone (which helps to explain that seventy percent Bill mentioned). There will be those who facilitate and those who catalyze and those who just stroke our hair as we fall apart. All of them are important to the process.

- Who in your life could help you begin to locate your spider if you took the risk of opening up to them?
- What is holding you back from allowing someone to help you through the rough spots of your journey?

BALDERDASH

Seeing what Sharon went through was not in my ball-park of what I was expecting to see and hear at OnSite. Also not in my ballpark was me being so active in someone else's healing. Sometimes I think we gloss over the power we have in other people's stories and the power others can have in ours. And sometimes it's from someone we least expect.

Remember how I told my daughter Seanna how I was going to summer camp for adults? I didn't know it at the time I said it, but it was true in more ways than one. For instance, we had a camp cook (chef). We had our camp counselors (therapists). We even had a sort of camp dad. When we showed up, Bill was quick to point out that once the staff went home for the night, there was a staff that would still be there for us at night. Maybe if we needed a hug or had a scary dream, I suppose? I thought this was a little funny. I'm a forty-year-old man. I think I'll be okay. Our night staff was a man named Dex. Dex was the guy who took our phones on that first evening we were there, so I was already not fond of him. All I knew was that he was the guy who knew where Instagram was, and he wouldn't let me go there. Dex was also in charge of the evening activities. One night was movie night. One night was game night. See, it *is* like camp for adults!

Game night. We were playing Balderdash. If you've never played, this is a game where a word is read that nobody knows the definition for. Everyone writes down a made-up definition with the goal of convincing everyone that your definition is the real definition. Someone then reads everyone's fake definitions along with the real definition mixed into the bunch. Everyone then votes on which definition they think is the real definition, and if more people vote for your fake definition than the real definition, you win that round!

I loved this game. I always had. It wasn't until I was three rounds in and destroying everyone in the game that something inside of me triggered. It hit me from the back without me even expecting it. I lost my breath and immediately got up and walked away.

"Carlos? You okay?" someone asked as I was almost running away. I didn't reply. I just knew that I needed to stop playing that game. It had for some reason turned from being a fun game into a game highlighting one of my biggest childhood wounds. It was a game in which the biggest liar was the biggest winner. And it sucked the breath right out of me.

I was sobbing on a stump next to the horse fence behind my cabin for several minutes when I heard footsteps. I tried to pull it together. I'm an ugly crier.

"Carlos? You okay, buddy? It's Dex."

The man who took my phone from me.

"Yeah. I'm fine. I just got overwhelmed for some reason. Just needed a break," I replied.

"You know there is never just 'some reason.' Wanna talk about it?" Dex replied.

The last thing I wanted to do was therapy on game night. Especially therapy from a guy who's not a therapist. Dex was just the night-watch guy. I'm sure his job was simply to make sure that none of us snuck away in the middle of the night to smoke or something.

"I'm okay, man. Thanks for checking in," I answered.

Dex began to walk away.

The truth? I was farther from okay than I had been the entire three days I'd been at OnSite. A board game suddenly triggered something inside of me that I didn't like. The truth was that I was good at Balderdash because I am a good liar. The truth was that I did need to talk to Dex at that moment.

"Dex! Can you come here, man? I'm actually not okay." I yelled out. But he was too far away to hear me now. I was gonna have to get off my butt and walk to Dex. That may seem like nothing, like the easy thing to do. But if you have ever been only a few feet from help and not felt the strength to go get it, you understand. Sometimes when help was staring you in the face, and you rejected it, you have to get up and go get it. And so I did.

Dex didn't bat an eyelash when I asked to talk. And honestly, there was something about him *not* being a therapist that made it a little easier.

I went all in. Telling him about how that stupid little game triggered something inside of me. Telling him all about being a kid and lying about accepting Jesus. Telling him about how I can't seem to get over the fact that I feel like a freaking fraud at this thing called life. Telling him how I seem to always rub crap on my blessings. We went from zero to hero in a hurry. Poor guy.

"It's not just you," he said. And then he sat still just staring at me. As if those four words were supposed to fix me. "Look around. Do you see what's going on here? All of them. All of your new friends feel like frauds too. And you know the good news? None of you are. None of us are. We all know right from wrong. And we all feel like we choose wrong more than we choose right. But just because you are good at Balderdash, Carlos, doesn't make you a fraud." I was stunned. It wasn't the most enlightening conversation I have had in my life. It wasn't laced with tweetable quotes. But it was true. And for some reason, when I looked around at everyone gathered around the tables with board games on them, I suddenly saw it. I saw humanity for what it is. A bunch of imperfect people trying their best to live a good life and make good decisions. And it gave me breath. As it should you.

Sometimes, on some issues, we operate in grey areas, but the majority of us have no trouble discerning the difference between right and wrong. There is something deep inside a human being that allows us to differentiate good and bad. We intrinsically know because we all have the fabric of the King of Kings woven inside of us. God Himself created each and every one of us, and I believe that is why, even when we don't know Jesus, we are able to make those judgments.

So why is it that we cannot freaking stop doing bad?

Why is it that yesterday, when driving past that homeless man, I knew in my heart I should have talked to him, but I didn't? Why is it that when my wife drove up with a mini-van filled with groceries that needed to be carried in, I sat on my phone watching a show, hoping she would bring them up all alone and not bother me for help? (Obviously, that didn't go down as I was hoping.)

The struggle is *real*.

But the struggle isn't always massive. Wanting to watch another episode of *Stranger Things* on my iPhone instead of helping Heather with the groceries isn't a massive moral failure, but it is a selfish choice.

Paul talks about this struggle in Romans 7:15–17 (CSB):

> For I do not understand what I am doing, because I do not practice what I want to do, but I do what I hate. Now if I do what I do not want to do, I agree with the law that it is good. So now I am no longer the one doing it, but it is sin living in me.

That is a lot of dos and don'ts and want to dos but can'ts. It's almost too much. At first glance, it would seem as though Paul is telling us—in the most eloquent way possible—we are screwed. The Carlos translation reads this way:

> I'm so confused. Why in the world can't I do what I know is right, and why am I always doing what is wrong? Relax. It's not you. It's sin. But does that mean I can just chalk this up to, "Oh, well, I guess I'm just gonna sin forever"? I *want* to do good. I *feel* that deep inside. But lookie there. I just chose

bad again. *Ugh!* I know God is inside of me, but I also know that sin is inside of me. And so continues the freaking battle.

I know. Somebody please nominate me for Bible translator of the year.

But you get it. It's a battle. It is not going to end. If we can come to the understanding and acceptance that it is not going to end, then we are close to the answer to this battle inside of our hearts. And the answer lies in the next chapter of Romans (8:1–2, 11 CSB):

> Therefore, no condemnation now exists for those in Christ Jesus, because the Spirit's law of life in Christ Jesus has set you free from the law of sin and of death. . . . And if the Spirit of Him who raised Jesus from the dead lives in you, then He who raised Christ from the dead will also bring your mortal bodies to life through His Spirit who lives in you.

Thank you, Jesus. And my translation: Gaze at God. Glance at life. That's it. We are all going to have this battle raging inside of our hearts. We are all going to have to face this battle between flesh and spirit on a daily basis. But instead of staring straight into the face of flesh, look up. Stare up. *Gaze* up. When you do that, "He who raised Christ from the dead will also bring your mortal bodies to life through His Spirit who lives in you."

Let's simplify this even more.

During my convo with Dex, he asked me a simple question.

"Can you tell me a time this past week when you made the right decision? When you made the choice of light over darkness?"

The first thing that came to mind was supersilly.

"I was gonna order a burrito at Chipotle but ordered a salad instead?" It felt dumb coming out of my mouth, but I said it anyways.

"Perfect!" Dex responded. "Now another!"

"I chose to get up at 5:30 a.m. to work out instead of sleeping in. I wanted to do that every morning. I only pulled it off one morning."

"We aren't talking about every morning. We are talking about that one morning," Dex continued.

"I did the dishes after everyone had gone to bed even though it's the kids' chore. I know Heather likes to wake up to a clean kitchen."

"I responded back to an email I had been avoiding like the plague. I took Pope out at midnight when I knew he needed to go to the bathroom instead of just ignoring him and sleeping. I took my oldest daughter, Sohaila, to Waffle House on a date and left my phone at home. I got the oil changed in the Jeep and saved us a few bucks with a coupon I searched for online. I didn't respond to a very attractive, probably fake Twitter profile when they complimented my Bible knowledge. I called my dad on the way home from a meeting when I didn't really want to talk. I only had one beer at the dinner party last Wednesday instead of having four." And I kept going. I probably talked for five straight minutes. What started as a chore suddenly turned into a waterfall of goodness from the life of Carlos. My life had suddenly become inspirational. And in a matter of minutes,

I began to see myself as a good guy who occasionally made wrong choices instead of a bad guy who occasionally made good choices. Dex had flipped my script. Dex, this night shift Resident Assistant, the guy who had my phone and my internet; that guy. He made me realize that just like Paul said in the Romans verse a few pages back . . . "If the Spirit of Him who raised Jesus from the dead lives in you, then He who raised Christ from the dead will also bring your mortal bodies to life through His Spirit who lives in you."

That is the good stuff! We may *feel* like there ain't a thing we can do right. But just think about it for a second. Start naming the goodness inside of you. It's there, and there is *way* more of it than you could ever imagine. You just have to start saying it out loud. Slowly begin to replace that lie and watch breath enter your lungs like it hasn't in a long time. A few minutes later, I found myself back at the Balderdash table crushing my opponents without an ounce of regret.

What Secrets Are You Keeping?

Let's start replacing some of the overwhelming lies in your life. The lie that I was a fraud and only capable of doing good every once in a while was *more massive* than I could even imagine. But that's just it. It's a lie. And all it took was some quick contemplation.

- Look back at the last week. What are the good things that you pulled off? When did light win for you over darkness?
- Think of at least three people in your life whom you

love and care for. What are some ways in which you have been light to them over the years?

- Pay attention in the next few weeks. Notice times when you may overreact to a situation or become more emotional than the situation warrants. Here is where you ask Jesus, *What is this? Why am I reacting this way? Stay with me, Jesus. Show me why.*

THE LABYRINTH

Our smartphones can get in the way of living life. When we handed our devices over to Dex on that first evening, I imagined that it was more about being fully present than anything else. And yes, this was one of the desired outcomes of not having a phone in my pocket. I was fully there. I was not focused on the outside world. That made sense. But there was an outcome of being phoneless that I was not prepared for: the absolutely mind-blowing decibel level in which silence existed. The silence was *so* loud. We had no television. We had no laptops. We had no smartphones. We had no newspapers. We had no *idea* what was going on outside of Camp OnSite. It was exactly why I had so many come to Jesus moments at camp when I was a kid in the '80s. There were no distractions. I'm romanticizing our pre-smartphone days just a little bit, but you don't have to have a PhD in sociology to understand that something has happened to our attention spans. Something has happened to our ability to process, well, anything.

I noticed right away that the silence at OnSite was

helping untangle things in my brain. It was loosening knots and tangles in my soul. Things were becoming clearer a lot faster than they normally do. It was taking me less time to process some new truths than it ever would have back home. Makes sense. Untangling makes sense. But you know what didn't make sense at the time? Silence was also doing some major tangling. As much as the silence was helping me with the knots in my heart that I had been attempting to untangle for years, it was creating new knots. Knots inside my heart that I wasn't really ready for. It was taking some truths that I never doubted and making me doubt just a little. Truths that I always believed. This happens to us in life. Not normally at the pace it did in my little Narnia of therapy that OnSite was, but it happens.

For those of you who had an incredibly Steven Spielberg-ET-esque childhood, you know what I'm talking about—the childhood straight out of all the feel-good '80s blockbusters where parents love each other and you could ride your bike as far as the sidewalk traveled. All of your friends let you borrow their Transformers or Cabbage Patch Dolls whenever your heart desired. It was Heaven. It was life. It was true. Life was good, and then you grew up. When that happened, for some reason, what was true about life as a child was no longer true. Your marriage may be falling apart. Your healthy body may be failing you. Your kids may be making choices that contradict the values you raised them to have.

So you ask: Was the truth of your childhood and the life you knew not true? Or is it just not true anymore?

Or how about this? You grew up in church. You loved Jesus with all your heart. He was your joy and guide. He was the answer to all of your problems. And then one day you woke up and couldn't seem to find Him. He used to be there for you all the time, but now, somehow, He is silent. You give your heart the benefit of the doubt, but you still find silence. What happened? He used to be loud and now He isn't. Does that make His loudness a lie? Was it ever Him to begin with? Truth doesn't seem like truth anymore.

A State Farm insurance commercial asks this question: "What if we woke up one day, and everything just stopped going wrong? No more accidents? No more fires? No more emergencies? No more bad anything?" In the commercial it shows a scene of an intersection with forty cars speeding through with no method to their madness, and there is a kid riding his bike through the middle of it with no worries and without getting hit. Unfortunately, this is what we expect to get when we say yes to Jesus. And although it may feel like this for a hot minute, this isn't truth—at least not this side of Heaven. It won't ever be true, but man do we want it to be true. So often we come out on the other side of a tragedy completely giving up on God because our feelings do not match our dreams. But this unraveling of truth, although gut-wrenching and terrifying, is the beginning of getting to real truth—a truth that doesn't depend on your feelings and that will allow you to face your spider with strength, not fight it with a nerf gun.

For me, this unraveling, gut-wrenching, terrifying moment happened on day three of OnSite.

Every morning, we woke up and had our "meditation time" before breakfast, but after coffee. There was no smoking at OnSite and no drugs—except for coffee. That is a legal drug there, and every morning, almost every single person gathered around one coffee pot. It was in the old

Gone With the Wind house kitchen. Forty humans, beat up and battered from the emotional work of the day before, would show up and stand in line for the liquid drug. And slowly but surely, Folgers drip coffee returned hope to life. I swear it tasted better than the best pour-over coffee I've ever had at Crema. (Well, until I was able to get back to Crema.) Isn't it funny how when you don't have options, that option suddenly tastes like manna from Heaven?

For the first two mornings, our meditation had been in the big room where we all gathered for our large group time. We started off with a breathing exercise that, without the coffee, would have put me right back to sleep. After calming ourselves, Bill began to read meditations to us and take us to places in our minds and hearts we probably hadn't been to in a long time, if ever. I've never been much of a meditator, but I was growing to like it. It was a departure from anything I had normally done. I had been taught to pray when I woke in the morning, and I guess this was a sort of prayer, but not the kind I was used to. When I pray, I talk. This was more listening.

But this morning, after we got to the room, Bill declared to us all that we would be taking a walk. Oh, I thought, a cute nature walk. It was 7:30 a.m. on a late summer Tennessee morning, which meant it was already spiritual. The morning fog had yet to lift from the hills, so we were walking in a sort of mist. Single file, past the horseshoe pit and around the first set of cabins. Nobody said a word. Remember the silence I was talking about earlier? She was singing. It was absolutely beautiful. The property was fifteen miles from the nearest highway, so there wasn't any traffic in the distance. No hum of cars or trains rumbling by. It was just our feet tapping the slick grass beneath them. A few times the horses to our left neighed and made other horseish type sounds, as if to say good morning as we walked by them. But it was so quiet. And it was so right.

"We are heading toward a labyrinth, friends. For those of you not familiar with a labyrinth, it isn't a maze. A maze may have multiple ways in or out. A labyrinth has a single direct path from beginning to end with many turns. So although it may look like a maze, it's not." Okay, I liked this. All the hippie was spilling out of me at this moment. I was in.

Bill continued, "When we get to the labyrinth, we will slowly, with a steady pace, single file, enter the labyrinth. As you enter, think about God—who God is to you. Once you have that in mind, with every turn you take in the labyrinth, begin to let go of something you have held true about God that you need to get rid of. Just begin to strip away all of the stuff God does not need from your heart and soul. With every turn, take something and place it to the side. When you get to the center of the labyrinth, we will all be there together with nothing but whomever 'God' is in your life."

What in the world would I need to get rid of? God was God. He was and is everything to me. But just as everything else I had experienced so far that week, I dove in head first.

If you are over thirty-five and reading this book, the word *labyrinth* may take you back to the psychedelic puppet movie with the same name starring David Bowie. It had a massive labyrinth with walls as big as a house. That wasn't the case with this one. This labyrinth was made of stones not bigger than our feet. It was a path, not a maze. It was at the top of a hill looking over a field. We all got to the top of the hill and stared silently at the majesty that was this Tennessee morning. It was so quiet. So peaceful. So still. The mist was still heavy and the dew lingered. You could have heard a pin drop. Suddenly there was sound. From somewhere in the woods, we heard the long, drawn out sound of a bagpipe. Just the drone. You know the one— the low hum.

I was captured by the sound. This place had more tricks up its sleeve than I had anticipated. Bravo, Bill. I liked the bagpipe music being pumped through the speakers in the forest. Nice touch. The singular note soon turned into a melody with a drum beat on every second and fourth beat. But the sound was getting closer. Not louder, but closer. Bill told us to begin the exercise. And so we began to enter the labyrinth, one by one. As I entered, I saw him. A figure appearing from the woods. He was wearing a kilt, playing a bagpipe, and suddenly I was in *Braveheart*. *A real bagpipe player? This place is magic.* As he got closer, I recognized the familiar tune. I was entranced by the melody. The words were on my lips, and I sang along in a whisper, "Amazing grace, how sweet the sound / That saved a wretch like me. / I once was lost, but now I'm found, / Was blind, but now I see."

The grass that our feet had been pacing across now turned to dirt. The path which was outlined with stones was now a little bit crunchier. But I think they designed it that way on purpose. Something tangible happens inside you when you step off something soft and onto something hard. With every turn of the labyrinth, I felt a sense of freedom. I was dropping things that I held that I no longer needed. A bad church experience at the first turn. That moment I was told that I wasn't a capable Christian leader by someone I really looked up to. I'm sure they meant it in love but, man, I had no idea how much it hurt. Pause. Breathe. Now, just like Bill said, lay it down. And so I did. A lie I believed about God at the second turn. That God had favorites. That for some reason He didn't believe that I could handle being a Christian leader. Oh wow. That stung. And look how closely it's tied into that moment at the last turn. I've got to let this go. It's not true. So I do. My pace began to slow as I approached every turn. I wanted to make sure that I unloaded what was weighing me down in my faith. I could see only a few turns into this exercise how freeing this was going to be. As I continued toward the center, I literally was feeling the freedom of getting rid of these lies that were not necessary in my faith.

Somewhere behind me, Bill called out to us. "Now, listen guys. When you get to the center, you will have only your God, but on the way back out of the labyrinth, literally, at every turn, I want you to put back in place *only* what is necessary in your faith. Leave behind what you don't need. You can put some stuff back on if you want, but know that you're making a choice."

I wasn't to the center of the labyrinth yet and still had several turns to make. This small bit of information from Bill made me wonder. What else was I going to let go of? I had this calm yet piercing thought: let go of everything but God. I didn't know what that meant, but on the very next turn I said out loud to myself, "Okay, I believe in Jesus, but for just a minute, I'm going to put that to the side because it's a hard one. The whole raising from the dead thing. I know I believe it, but for just a second, let me rid myself of anything hard to believe in. Just get to God." Dangerous? Sure. But, for the sake of the exercise, I put Jesus to the side. The next turn I said the same thing about the Holy Spirit. I mean, the Trinity is real to me, so it's not like I was actually putting Jesus and the Holy Spirit to the side. But, figuratively, I needed to get to the simple root of who God the Father is.

I started feeling some anxiety the closer I got to the center. I mean some real, tangible anxiety. When I got to the center of the labyrinth, I remember specifically feeling like I still had God. And God was good. And God was in control even though I felt very out of control. It was an incredibly strange feeling, and it was a long few minutes in the center of the labyrinth before Bill told us we should start making our way back out again. I could not wait because I was ready to get Jesus and the Holy Spirit and the Bible and all of the stuff that makes my faith work back on. Turn number one. "Okay, I put Jesus back." Nothing. I felt nothing. "Jesus. I believe in you. I think. Jesus? Are you real? *Jesus*?" The panic began to flood over me in ways I hadn't felt in years. "Holy Spirit. Come. Come, Holy Spirit. Come, please!" Nothing. Nada. What was happening? With every turn, I got closer to the outside of the labyrinth, and nothing was sticking. Bill said we could put back on everything we needed, but *nothing* was sticking. I began to weep. I felt so lost. By the time I got out, I sprinted to Bill and Nancy who were standing on the edge.

"Hey, Bill. I don't know what's happening. I'm kinda freaking out. I can't seem to reconvince myself that Jesus is real. He is real. I mean, I think He is. He is, right? What's happening?" I was in a full-blown panic. Nancy grabbed my hand and walked me to the side.

"Breathe, Carlos. Take a deep breath. Remember, trust the process. Celebrate the miracles."

"Nancy. This isn't a miracle. I don't like this process. I can't go home and tell my wife that I don't believe in Jesus anymore! What is happening?" I quietly yelled. (Yes, that is possible.)

"Maybe you never really believed in the first place."

What was this mythical spiritual mumbo jumbo she was talking about? Somebody told me Jesus was real. I sang songs about Jesus being real every week. And then the thought hit me. *Maybe I always just assumed Jesus was real. I never really found out for myself.*

I sprinted back to my cabin and grabbed the only thing I knew could bring me peace in this panic-filled moment: my Bible.

I opened that bad boy up and started flipping. I wanted and needed some sort of anchor. But you know what? It all felt like fluff. It all felt like made-up stories. *What was happening?* Was everything I ever believed about God an absolute lie? Was everything I ever believed about Jesus a sham? Had I been duped? Absolutely everything about my faith was being turned upside down in a matter of hours. I was scared. I was confused. I didn't know what was happening. I felt as though my faith was a lie. I was screaming at God from my bed in my cabin. I felt so alone. I just wanted to go home, back to before I experienced this confusion. Who was I without the faith I had built my life on?

But the truth was, I was just beginning to find Him. Jesus never left. The Holy Spirit never left. They were there.

I just had to find them for myself. Instead of letting songs and sermons be my guide, I was going to have to find them in the silence. And the new truth that was coming was greater than any truth I had ever known before.

What If It's Actually God Unraveling Our Beliefs in Order to Rebuild Them?

Facing a crisis of faith is not uncommon. Many of us go through this experience. It's not only okay, it's important. We can grow up either having a faith ingrained in us by our families and communities, or we can grow up with misconceptions about faith as an outsider. Neither of these is real or personal. We often have to unpack the baggage we've carried through life around this issue so we can start anew with a different set of essentials that are what we really need to take with us on the journey.

- What sort of experiences are stretching your view of God?
- What does the current state of your relationship with God look like?
- How can you disturb and disrupt your relationship with God so that you get uncomfortable?

❉

THE SATAN DUPLEX

The morning after I had accidentally stopped believing in Jesus, I woke up feeling like I had been to the final round in a prize fight. Everything was sore. I was exhausted. It was as though I had been in a physical battle as opposed to a spiritual battle. But then again, maybe those two aren't separated by as much as we think. I picked up my Bible and opened it again . . . *Sigh* . . . Just as fluffy as it was yesterday. Stick a fork in my faith. It was done. And as depressing as that sounds, it was true. All my years growing up in the church . . . working full-time for the church . . . writing songs for the church . . . That faith was gone. I didn't know where the outcome of this spiritual battle royale was taking me, but I knew it wasn't to the safe spiritual sauna I had been relaxing in before. No, I knew I could never go back there again. So where would I go? How would I find my faith again?

When I was twenty-one, I was in one of the darkest seasons of my life. I was in my fifth year at Berry College in Rome, Georgia, and I was a mess. I was a lost soul looking for any sort of validation. But I wasn't necessarily looking to fix myself. I had a job. I hadn't been expelled (yet). I had a condo. I had a girlfriend. People from afar still saw me as having it together. But, man, was I not together—drinking heavily whenever I could, sleeping till noon, and missing work all the time. I didn't have a name for it, although now I can look back and see that I was suffering from heavy depression and anxiety. I was 2,500 miles away from my parents. I felt so alone. I had slowly but surely pushed away all my friends.

It was a pretty scary and sad time. Sad is the easy word to define here. But I was also scared, and that word is a little harder to nail down. What did I have to be scared of? Nobody was after me. I had parents who loved me. But I felt this fear. I didn't know why. It just lingered.

"For our struggle is not against flesh and blood, but against the rulers, against the authorities, against the powers of this dark world and against the spiritual forces of evil in the heavenly realms" (Ephesians 6:12).

Man, I wish I had known more about this struggle back then. I didn't. But I was about to be right in the middle of it. It was a Wednesday night in the middle of summer. Somehow I had figured out a way to extend going to a four-year liberal arts school into almost six years. My girlfriend had broken up with me the day before. Looking back, I don't blame her. I was a hot mess. The week before, I had been fired from my job at Buffalo's. I had stopped showing up. And on this particular Wednesday, I just sat in my condo and cried. *How had my life ended up so sad, and why did I have this feeling of fear?* I wasn't telling anyone about my struggle. I was determined to figure it out on my own.

That night, after spending the entire day inside my duplex, I remember feeling even more fear. It was kinda spooking me a bit. I checked all the closets to make sure nobody was in them. (Don't fool yourself; you've done this before.) I remember even praying a shotgun prayer before I fell asleep. It was a heart cry loaded with, *Dear Lord, help me not feel this way when I wake up.*

I woke up around 3:00 a.m. The feeling that came over me can only be described as dark. I had never felt so scared in my life. I pulled the covers over my head and started praying.

Dear God, I pray that You make this stop. I'm so sorry. I promise I'll behave, God. Please. Whatever is in here, make it leave!

I knew nothing was in my room, but I knew something was in my room. The darkness was darker than just the lights being off and the sun yet to rise. Something was up. And that something was dark. My window was open, and the curtains were flapping a bit more than normal. I was freaking out. After about two minutes of nonstop prayer, I knew I needed to be rescued from whatever was happening in my duplex that night. I needed my dad, so I jumped out of bed and ran to the kitchen to call him.

Yes, I had to get out of bed to call him. The phone was fifteen feet away. This was before cell phones.

Why would I call my dad? Because although I didn't know much about this whole dark, evil, and spiritual warfare stuff, I was most certain that I was in it right then. And I was sure that my dad would know how to help me out of it.

It was midnight in Fresno, California, where he lived. Would he even hear the phone ring when I called? I hoped so. I flipped the light switch on, and as I reached for the phone to dial his number, it rang. Read that again: Right as I was reaching for the telephone, it rang. And it rang. And it rang.

I had never, nor have I since, felt as scared as I was in that moment.

What was going on? Was I going to pick up the phone and hear the voice of Skeletor on the other end?

Everything froze. I slowly reached for the phone, picked it up, and put it to my ear.

"Carlos, it's dad. It's okay. I love you. I was woken up to pray for you, and I want you to know it's okay. It's time to come home, son. It's time to come home."

I grew up in a Southern Baptist home where we sang hymns and nobody lifted their hands in worship. I didn't grow up in a house where we talked about this spiritual warfare stuff. I didn't grow up in a church where people fought against demons and things that go bump in the night.

But you know what I did grow up in? I grew up in a home where I would seldom go a day without seeing my father on his knees with the Father. My dad was a giant. And apparently he had direct access to the Holy Spirit 'cause things just got *crazy*.

You see, that is the sort of moment that you can't ignore. You can't forget.

Guess what I did.

I didn't say a thing. I just cried. My dad prayed for me and then hung up. Then I started packing. I packed up everything I could fit into my Honda Accord. I mean *everything*. And the next morning when my Vietnamese neighbors I shared a wall with woke up, I let them know they could have everything I'd left in my duplex. "What happened? Where are you going?" they asked me.

"I'm going to be with my dad because whatever he has, I want it. I want all of it." And I drove west from Rome, Georgia, heading toward Fresno, California. I had no idea at the time that I would not return to Georgia. But I did know that I needed to sit under my father's roof again. I needed to pay attention to whatever I had been ignoring for so long. I believed it now. Yeah, it took a crazy moment like that for me to believe. And even still, to this day, sometimes I think things like, *It was a coincidence. Every once in a while, the stars align. What are the chances?* And, every time, the response I get back from God is, "Yeah, Carlos, what *are* the chances?"

The battle is real, my friends. The sooner we accept that, the sooner our spider killing can begin. And the sooner the spider dies.

How Are the Spiders Working against You, Playing into the Spiritual Warfare?

You may have heard the saying, "The greatest trick the Devil ever pulled was to make you think he doesn't exist." When we sit in denial of the reality of spiritual warfare, we are denying the enemy exists and that he is trying to distract us from the work God wants us to do to clean out the cobwebs and get rid of our spiders. So much of the struggle we face comes from the enemy feeding us lies and us buying into them. The sooner you stop allowing him to have control, the sooner you can get on to living without cobwebs in your life.

- When was the last time God blew your mind?
- Have you ever felt darkness from the enemy?
- Is there someone you respect who walks with God? Send them a message and ask to get together for coffee or lunch.

FROM CRAVING TO COBWEB

One of the things that Bill kept saying all week long was that seventy percent of everything we learned that week would be from someone else's story. I remember not believing him when he first said it and then a hundred percent believing him by day two. Sometimes we are *so* introspective that we forget that our eyes and ears are for more than just consuming Netflix episodes.

Obviously, from Sharon's story a few chapters back, you can see how *massively* we can learn from others. Every morning around the one, single coffee pot that was brewing the nectar of the gods, we could see it happening. People learning from each other's stories. I only spent about three hours of this entire week talking about my issues. Three hours of me yapping about me! The rest of the week was spent listening to others and their stories. So maybe I can correct Bill for a moment. It's actually not seventy percent. According to Siri, the incredible personal assistant that lives on my iPhone, there are 168 hours in a week. So using the example of my three hours out of a week's worth of therapy, we learned from someone else's story 98.2143% of the time and only 1.7857% from our own story. You're welcome.

Our therapists weren't there to share their stories. They were there to help us pull out ours. And that they did with an artistry normally saved for spaces like the Sistine Chapel. But every once in a while, Nancy would sneak a bit of her story into the pot. My goodness. What a driven woman. She obviously had wounds, but those wounds were so enviable. I was sitting there thinking, I wish those were my wounds. They seemed so neat and tidy. You know those people, the ones whose sins seem so sweet. They don't struggle with pornography or drug addiction. They struggle with balancing their budget three out of twelve months. Those people. The ones who have this living thing down. Nancy seemed like that to me. She was a driven and accomplished woman. She reminded me a lot of my wife. Strong. Determined. Focused. Caring. Brave. On day three, Nancy was talking about her life, and my mind wandered back to a moment in the car a few weeks prior with my wife.

My wife is incredible. Her family is incredible. When we first started dating, I would get overwhelmed with the amount of stuff her family knew how to do and how little I knew. She grew up with a dad who fixed absolutely everything. Everything. There isn't anything on the planet that man can't fix with a screwdriver and some duct tape. Come to think of it, he looks awfully similar to MacGyver. The man does not encounter a project he cannot figure out. I recently heard the phrase, "Everything is figureoutable." This is my wife's mantra. She figures everything out.

At *every* dinner party she cooks for, Heather hears, "Heather! This _____ is incredible! Can I have the recipe?"

to which she responds that there was no recipe. She just figured it out as she made it. She knew what she wanted in the end and just instinctively worked toward it.

My wife also has the gift of hospitality. It's a gift from God—a desire given to her by God. The dinner parties she puts on at our house make Pinterest buzz with excitement. Every time I mention one of her parties on social media, I get slammed with people asking me to take photos of every angle of her skills. People feel valued and loved by Heather when she uses the gifts God has given her. How can they not when someone pours that much time and energy into something for them? This gift my wife has makes people feel like they belong to something bigger. It is truly special.

But back to my memory while Nancy was talking. I was thinking of how Nancy's wounds seem less heinous than mine—that I envied her problems—when I remembered it. Awhile back, on a long drive somewhere, I had the bright idea of trying to convince Heather that her passion should be turned into a business of sorts. She could become the next Martha Stewart! "C'mon, baby. You could help the family out financially while still doing what you love!" It just made sense, but she wasn't into my idea. Like, at all.

"Carlos, the second it becomes a business, it's no longer fun." Being the entrepreneurial addict that I am, I could not understand this response. But I could tell it wasn't gonna happen. So the conversation shifted.

"So babe. Why do you do it then? Why do you create all these incredible moments for people? You do it all the time. Is it just out of the pure joy it gives you?" There was a long pause. I could tell she was thinking really hard about the question and choosing her words carefully. "Yes, I love it.

Yes, I love to make people feel loved. But, you know what? I've never realized it before now, but it also makes me feel loved."

Wow. There was a moment. We all desire to feel loved. This was a way she felt loved, and that wasn't a bad thing. But the more we explored this thought over the next few days, the deeper the conversation went. "I can't help but wonder if I stop throwing all these dinner parties, would anyone call me back?" she asked. "I wonder if I do this because I am actually trying to *control* love? Do you think I'm controlling love?" The thought grew bigger. The emotions tied to it grew bigger.

The next morning, Heather walked back in from her prayer time on the porch. "Two weeks. Two weeks is what He said."

"What who said?" I asked.

"God. This morning during my prayer time, I heard Him say two weeks. I'm not to reach out to any friends for two weeks. I won't ignore them if they reach out. But God wants me to get my complete and total fulfillment from Him for two weeks."

Heather went on to lay it out for me. Her desire—the God-given desire to host and cook and love people—had become a cobweb for her. It had become something she used in order to manipulate how she received love. She had been using her gifting and desire to feed the need she had for others' love. Mind. Blown.

I couldn't even imagine this being a problem. Who cares if people love you for what you do for them? But that's because it wasn't a problem for *me*. Just as many people can't understand why someone would look at porn for false intimacy, I couldn't understand how someone would feel bad for throwing dinner parties.

"Okay. God doesn't want you to throw dinner parties for two weeks. That's fine. He doesn't want you to call people for two weeks. That's fine. But how is that going to help?"

"I'm not exactly sure," she replied. "But I feel like God is actually telling me that even if nobody calls me or reaches out to me to hang out or go have a meal, *He* is enough. *He* is all I need."

Now we were heading toward the spider.

After a few more days of processing, Heather got to the spider.

Heather realized she had made an idol out of friendship, community, and the feelings of love she received from these things.

And the spider, the lie, was identified as: "I must *do* to be *loved*."

This was the lie. This was the spider.

The spider is the lie that spins the cobweb.

The cobweb is the medicator that offers false comfort through the lie.

As you start searching for your spiders, it's gonna take some work. It is. But there's good news. Heather was right: everything *is* figureoutable. There is Scripture that helps us understand this. Paul is talking to the church of Philippi when he tells them, "I am able to do all things through him who strengthens me" (Philippians 4:13 CSB).

See? Everything is figureoutable. Everything. Paul was talking to everyday people like you and me. Sure, athletes can draw inspiration from this verse and apply it to slam dunking over an opponent or shooting one to the top left corner of a soccer goal, but this verse is meant to help us with the everyday—the ordinary stuff that beats us down to the point that we would rather give up than press on. And I'm not saying just because it's ordinary that it's not big. I just don't want you to believe that Paul is speaking only to epic issues.

This spider-killing thing takes guts. It takes more strength than we have. You are going to reach a point in this journey when you want to quit—where giving up on trying to kill this spider seems like a really good option. You may be tempted to think you have lived this long with your spider so you may as well just coast through life. I get it.

Want to know how seriously I get it? I'm sitting in the front seat of my van with my laptop on my lap while Heather is driving north on some backcountry Wyoming road. Ever since I got serious about finishing this book, the attack has been *on*. Overwhelming, to the point of defeat. I had written about ten thousand words before I reread them, scrapped everything, and started over. I started over because I knew it was the right thing to do—to get real and honest and raw. And almost *to the minute*, the spiritual attacks began. Satan was not happy that I had taken this challenge more seriously to help other people find freedom. And suddenly, more than I have struggled with in years, anxiety reared its ugly head back into my life. The second I started rewriting, my anxiety started showing up in every way it could. And there have been plenty of times I had a *serious* conversation with God that went like this:

God, I can't do it. I know this is spiritual, but I'm so exhausted. If I stop writing this book, will it stop? If I stop writing this book, will the attacks slow down? I may need to give it a break.

But every time I tried, I would remember the verse from Philippians, not for the athletic power or for the bravery it should magically inject into my heart. I actually read it taking in the verse before it as well.

"In any and all circumstances I have learned the secret of being content—whether well fed or hungry, whether in abundance or in need . . ."

After that, Paul writes that we can do anything through Him who gives us strength. Now the game changes because you know that no matter your circumstance, no matter how you feel at the moment, and no matter what you are facing, you can do it. I can do it. Having this book in your hands is evidence enough. If I can press through debilitating fights with anxiety and *still* get this book to you, you can kill your spider too.

What Spiders Are Masquerading as Good Things in Your Life?

I'm going to give you a really bad pun, so get your groan ready. You might have a wolf spider in sheep's clothing lurking in your life. It's the thing that seems harmless, but is really pretty insidious in how it can unravel your relationships and other aspects of life. I'm going to ask you to write out the following sentence and fill in the blank:

My spider could be _____.

The spider will be a lie. It will be something you have been accepting as true, but ultimately isn't. Remember, it doesn't have to be this big, hairy, massive lie. Sometimes it is subtle. Sometimes it is small. Here are a few questions to help you get to it:

- Is your spider hidden in something that was a craving and has turned into a cobweb?
- Is it hidden in something that is a secret only you know?
- Is it hidden in plain sight because it's not sinister-looking to others?
- What is the lie you believe?

ANXIETY ATTACK

Mrs. Buchanan used to leave our fifth grade science class on a regular basis. She would stop teaching suddenly, smile awkwardly, and walk out of the room. It happened about once a week. "Panic attack," Chandra once whispered to me by way of explanation. Chandra Bishop was the teacher's pet. She knew *everything*. And apparently she knew that Mrs. Buchanan was having panic attacks. Chandra didn't announce it to the room; she just said it to me. "What's a panic attack?" I asked.

"She thinks she's going to die, so she has to go calm down."

That was the end of our discussion about the matter, and I remember clearly thinking at that moment that Mrs. Buchanan was crazy. Like three screws loose crazy. But the strange thing was that half the time Mrs. Buchanan would march back in within a few minutes and start teaching again; and the other half we wouldn't see her again for a few days.

I really thought she was crazy. And now I know she was

crazy. But I also know that we all are. You. Me. We are all crazy. My OnSite experience didn't pull this out of me. I'd known I was crazy for a while. But if there *was* something that OnSite was showing me, it was that the anxiety and depression I had struggled with for long was *not* the main issue. There was something else I needed to dig toward. They were the cobwebs of a spider somewhere in my head and my heart. I say head because I don't want anyone to ever say that anxiety is only a spiritual/soul matter. I understand that serotonin levels get whacked sometimes. I think it is a mixture of both.

I have always been a worrier. I remember lying in bed as a nine-year-old crying in my pillow because I was worried something would happen to my parents. There was absolutely nothing wrong with my parents. I simply worried. I worried they might get a divorce. I worried they would get in a car wreck. I worried they could be abducted by aliens. I know what you're thinking. I needed to be in therapy. Maybe. But the crazy thing is, there was no one moment that triggered this in me. I was just a kid who was more apt to worry than other kids. And it's not like I was all consumed by it. But it definitely came in waves.

Back in the '80s we all called it "worry." In 2017, it would probably be classified as anxiety. I was a happy kid, but I was an anxious kid.

The anxiety didn't interfere with my day-to-day. I had the classic suburban, middle class life—soccer practice, building forts with friends, putting pennies on the railroad tracks. I mean it was basically *Stand by Me* without discovering dead bodies and such. So I was a kid who struggled with worry. In the grand scheme of things, it was no big deal. Well, no big deal until the day it went from worry to war.

After my dad pulled the God-phone-call card on me at 3:00 a.m., I headed back to Fresno. Fresno was a blast because that's where I met Heather. The same Heather currently sitting next to me. She was eighteen and fresh out of high school. I was twenty-two and the opposite of whatever "fresh out of high school" meant.

I'll save you the Hallmark Channel screenplay of how we met, but just imagine me being played by 1990s Denzel Washington and Heather being played by 1990s Meg Ryan. It was a glorious time of dating. We fell madly in love and moved from Fresno, California, to Riverside, California, so I could finish up school at California Baptist University. We got married and had a baby.

Let's talk about my "career" for a second, because I know it's an issue to figure out what Carlos Whittaker has been doing all of these years he's been cleaning cobwebs.

I went to school and graduated with an Information Systems Management degree. This was in 2002. The dot com boom. I was working with a few guys starting a company and working as a leader at Sandals Church. I accidentally started leading worship. This was back in the day when the term "worship leader" was brand new. It wasn't something I went around bragging about. I just knew of Chris Tomlin and tried to act like him. I worked as the worship pastor at Sandals Church for nine years. Nine amazing, life-giving years. Life was so sweet. Our church was growing like crazy, and we were renting a little house on a hill overlooking Riverside, and soon we were expecting another bundle of joy.

As a happily married adult, I continued to struggle with anxiety, only it had taken shape in more sinister ways. It manifested in worries about health—like if I had a stomachache for more than six hours, I went to WebMD, and by hour seven I'd diagnosed myself with colon cancer.

But it was not just my mind being consumed with worry. There were physical manifestations: heart palpitations, shaking fingers, lack of sleep, lack of appetite, dizzy spells. But all of this was still manageable.

I was the worship pastor at Sandals, which basically meant I sang on Sundays and tried to sound good enough not to get fired.

On one particular Sunday—no different from any regular old Sunday—I woke up at 6:00 a.m., drove to Starbucks, ordered a venti skinny hazelnut latte, and headed to church. The band would rehearse, we would pray, and then it was service time. On this particular Sunday, we were meeting in the California Baptist University Theatre. I can't remember why, but I do remember that it wasn't our typical Sunday gathering spot. I think our first song was "Praise Song" by Third Day and Rich Mullins, and the second was "Jesus, Lover of My Soul" by Hillsong. And then we came to song number three. I remember it clearly. It was called "Salvation" by Charlie Hall. I loved the song. It was a song that was on the edge of what modern worship music was about to become. We had taken one pass through the verse and were just getting to the chorus. I remember it as if it were yesterday. For a second, absolutely everything went black. I almost felt as though I was going blind. And then poof. Everything came back into view. I remember thinking, *I need to breathe. Maybe I'm not breathing right.* Then it happened again. Black. This time in spots over the crowd. I remember specifically feeling like my heart was about to bust out of my chest. It wasn't hurting, but it was racing as if I'd just sprinted fifty yards. I looked to my right to my bass player Rod Merrit. I gave him a look that scared him. He mouthed back to me, "Are you okay?"

I didn't know what was happening. Was I dying? While I was leading worship? I went black again, and this time I stumbled backward. I put down my guitar as the band kept playing. No one in the crowd was aware of the situation, but my band was. I looked at them and said, "Keep playing," as I walked off stage. Nathan, one of the pastors on staff with me, ran to my side, "Hey, man. What's wrong? You okay?"

"I think I'm having a heart attack," I told him. I didn't know what else could have been causing me to black out, make my heart race, and make me feel so miserable. I sat on a sofa backstage, and Nathan calmly walked up to my microphone and asked if there was a doctor in the room.

I don't remember his name. I just remember he was calm. He took my pulse, asked me a few questions, and looked in my eyes.

Then he said something that would change my life forever: "Carlos, you aren't having a heart attack. I think you're having a panic attack."

Hold please. What? What did that mean? It was 2004, and churches weren't yet hip to the mental health crisis. I looked up at him and said, "Okay."

They walked me to my car. Heather had run to the nursery to get our baby Sohaila and then she got in the car. "You okay, baby?" she asked me. I just started weeping. I didn't know if I was okay. I didn't know if I was gonna be okay. I would much rather have had something be wrong with my heart at that moment. At least somebody could try to fix that as opposed to something wrong with my brain. I was so scared. I was shaking. And I know Heather was scared too.

Over the next few days, I couldn't even leave my driveway without the same level of panic coming up again. I would try to leave, but I would be reduced to tears and shake violently. The next day, I went to the doctor, hoping he would tell me something like, "You have an overactive _____. Take two of these and everything will be fine." But no. He had no answers. I was healthy, although my adrenaline was pumping like nobody's business.

So the doctor couldn't fix me. I figured God was going to have to. Ugh. I hated this part of faith—the part where you have to believe in something you do not see and trust something you cannot really hear. So I prayed. I prayed some heart-wrenching prayers, my friends. I cussed at God. I yelled at God. I screamed at God. I begged God. I wanted this feeling to go away. I wanted to wake up one morning and have the feelings of anxiety be gone. But they never did. They just stayed. And I slowly faded from the life I once knew. I stopped leading worship. I could barely get out of the house without having another panic attack. I was a prisoner in my own head. I pleaded, *Dear God. Where have you gone? Please Lord. Heal me.*

I suddenly couldn't do the one thing it seemed God had created me to do—lead people in worship. I couldn't even fathom the thought of ever getting back up on a stage again to sing. Was this the end of it? Was I done leading people to God's throne through music? How could I? I was completely embarrassed, and I was terrified. I was useless now. As a husband. As a pastor. As a friend. As a human. And obviously as a Christian, because I had begged God to come through for me and He just kept ignoring my prayers. He was gone. This was the lie. The spider.

My friends, this was as empty a space in life as I have ever been in. I was surrounded by friends and family, but felt as though I was in outer space. A million miles away. Whenever I try to explain what it feels like for me to struggle with anxiety and depression to someone who may not know or understand the feeling, I explain it like this:

Imagine for a moment you are surrounded by every single person in the world who loves you. They are celebrating who you are with a huge party. Everyone is waiting to talk to *you* and tell you that they love you and that you are amazing. Sounds awesome. Now imagine you are in a space suit. You can barely hear what anyone is saying and, although you are being hugged, you can't feel anything. In the midst of not being "alone" you feel completely alone.

I had lost heart. I was a twenty-nine-year-old, married with a kid and a good job, and I was going crazy.

Now, there is good news—maybe not at the end of this chapter, but in my story where I have fought and won. I am no longer owned by anxiety. Does it still play a part in my life? Absolutely. But after years of prayer, medication, therapy, and more prayer, I am on the other side of this battle. For those of you in need of closure, I'm okay. And so are you. But, listen, there is something that is massively important to this whole thing, something I didn't even see happening, something I did that I didn't know I did. And this, my friends, was the introduction of a spider into my life. I didn't even see it born. You'll find the clues a few paragraphs back.

These lines right here: "I was useless now. As a husband. As a pastor. As a friend. As a human. And obviously as a Christian, because I had begged God to come through for me and He just kept ignoring my prayers. He was gone."

I had agreed to some pretty massive and life-changing lies.

1. *I was useless.* This was huge and had so much impact on the next ten years of my journey. I made an agreement that I was useless when I wasn't able to get rid of my anxiety, so when I actually got rid of it, I still had that lie embedded in me.
2. *God was gone.* I had agreed with the lie that God had abandoned me. He was around no more. He had left the building, the building was on fire, and I was inside of it burning to the ground with it. He. Was. Gone.

This isn't something I consciously agreed to. Obviously, if you'd asked me if I believed those things I'd have argued against it, intellectually at least. I was so covered with the ripple effects of my panic attacks that I could barely breathe, much less study the impacts of the lies I had been creating with the enemy. And in my hour of feeling unworthy and small, I believed God had turned His back on me. And though I was able to crawl out of the hole of depression, those lies quietly grew inside me like cancer.

What Agreements Have You Made with the Enemy?

We can sabotage ourselves where our spiders are concerned. We are often the ones who let them in and allow them to start spinning their webs of deceit and destruction.

As we move forward, you will need some concrete steps for locating the birthplace of your spiders. We will get to those in the coming chapters, but for now, start down the road with that lie in your story.

- Have you bought into a lie about yourself, someone in your life, or God?
- Can you figure out why you agreed to it?

HATCHING SPIDERS

One afternoon group exercise at OnSite really took us outside our comfort zones. Not that we hadn't been there already this week—we had, but this was gonna take some extra work. Bill told us to find a partner—somebody of the same sex and not in our small group. So out of the forty people in the room, I had about fifteen guys to choose from. I'd made friends with this older gentleman from Atlanta named Tom. Remember, we were not allowed to tell people our last names or what we did professionally, but from what I could gather from Tom, he was either an arborist or a librarian. He gave the vibes that he cared about the little things and that he took great care of his family. And he had an epic white beard. I mean, *epic*. Santa epic. So, yeah, I chose Tom.

Bill stepped into the middle of the room. "Okay, guys and gals, here is what we are going to do. Each of you will share your entire life story with the person you have chosen. Grab a chair and sit face-to-face with your partner."

So we did. We dragged chairs across the floor and

rearranged sofas so we could follow his instructions. A nervous murmur filled the room. This was going to be intense.

At least we were doing it before lunch. There was the pecan pie to look forward to.

As soon as the room had settled down, Bill chimed in again. "Great. Now, hold the hands of your partner."

OK. Now we had crossed a line I didn't even know I had drawn. I was not going to hold Tom's hands. That was just weird.

"Once you have both of their hands in yours, stare into each other's eyes. Now, I know the hesitation many of you have with this. You can't even stare into your own family's eyes, much less a stranger's. But remember, trust the process. Celebrate the miracles."

I'd already nearly stopped believing in God by this point; what else did I have to lose? When I looked into Tom's eyes something incredible happened. Even before we began the crux of the exercise, I felt a calm I had not experienced in a long time. I felt peace. Tom's facial expression was soft. His eyes were red from the exhaustion of the week, yet clear with the hope and anticipation of what was to come. I didn't want to look away. So. Weird.

Bill continued, "Uncomfortable yet? Good. Okay, this is going to be a ten-minute exercise. For the first five minutes, one of you will tell the other one your life story. You will relive it. You will go back to the earliest moment you can remember, and for that five minutes I want you to remember as much as you can from your life. Moving forward in time slowly but surely. Here is the catch: You can only use your eyes to tell your story. That's it. This is not a verbal exercise. You tell your story just using your eyes."

What? I'm telling you, Bill had a way of laying down these crazy things without anyone even batting an eye. It sounded so strange, but it felt so right. Tom went first.

There was no background music playing. Nothing was there to take the edge off of the awkwardness of staring into a stranger's eyes for five minutes while they relived all the epic moments of their lives without saying a word. That's some crazy stuff, but again, it felt right. When Tom started, I could see happy wrinkles form at the sides of his eyes. He was trying not to smile, but his eyes couldn't help it. Then sadness formed in his brow. I could clearly see his pupils dilate and then constrict. At one point I saw tears form in his eyes. They took a solid minute to gather to the point where the tear in his left eye finally fell. But, although that tear formed when his eyes were at a place of broken-ness, I could tell that, by the time it fell, his eyes were at another part of his story—a joyful one, a hopeful one. Tom also squeezed my hands and then released his grip at several moments during his five minutes. It was as if his entire body was involved in his story, not just his eyes. By the time the five minutes were almost up, Tom's eyes weren't displaying much of anything. I couldn't necessarily tell if he was happy or if he was sad. He almost looked numb. Maybe that's why Tom was here. Maybe he wanted to feel life again. "Time's up!" Bill announced.

And just like that, I could see all of this pressure fall off of Tom's shoulders. He let out a sigh, almost a gasp. It was filled with life. All of it. I remember noticing a few people crying once Tom and I were snapped out of our trance. Some were visibly shaken up, like they, in no way shape or form, expected that to be such a powerful exercise. One woman actually stood up and ran out of the room. Man. What was I in for?

After giving us three or four minutes to gather our thoughts and regain our composure Bill piped up again, "It's time to switch roles. Ready? Let's begin."

And back I went, as far as my brain could wander. I am very clear on the first thing I thought about. It came from a photo I remember seeing in one of my parents' photo albums. It was me sitting on Santa's lap. I couldn't have been older than three years in the photo. I never remembered anything else about that photo. But you know what? In this moment, I actually remembered more than just the image from the picture. I remembered Santa's breath and how it stank! How in the world did details of the memory come flooding back to me? I have no idea, but it did. I also remember Tom's eyes while I was reliving this moment. He almost laughed out loud. I have no idea how the expression on my face looked, but it had to have been epic because Tom almost broke Bill's rule of not making any expressions back to the person delivering their story.

Onward I went. I was only seventeen seconds into this exercise. Maybe this was going to be possible after all. I continued my voyage across the span of my life. The next memory I encountered was not familiar to me at all. I could see the experience, almost taste it, it was so clear. But this was the first time I had recalled it out of the depths of my mind. I had zero clue where I was, but I knew I was around five years old. I was under a bed, though I didn't know whose bed it was. The more I thought about it, the more I could picture what was happening—and that it actually did happen. A friend was with me. She was about the same age as I was, and we both were naked. Our lips were chapped, and we were hugging. Here is where I broke one of Bill's rules. I looked away from Tom because I was kinda freaking out. What was this memory? How did it just randomly show up while I was looking into Tom's eyes?

I looked down and put my face in my hands. Tom whispered, "You okay buddy? It's okay. You wanna stop?"

I didn't respond. I just lifted my face out of my hands and looked back into Tom's eyes. They assured me. I felt safe enough to keep going. So I did. I remembered something very vividly. It was a feeling—a feeling of shame. The more I recalled and the more I remembered, the more I became certain that I felt shame at a very early age. But I thought to myself, *We were obviously just exploring sexuality. We were probably mimicking something we saw on some movie. What's there to be ashamed of when you are five years old with another five-year-old?* I was basically talking myself off of the ledge. Shame. I couldn't get rid of the shame I felt. Why was it there?

I kept trying to get past this thought to move onward through this voyage across my life. But I was stuck on this memory. What was happening? Why was I stuck? I must have been hugging and kissing another five-year-old. I remembered my lips were chapped, but that entire narrative went out the window when I remembered something else. I could tell Tom was extremely concerned and could see that I was stuck.

"We can stop, Carlos," he whispered to me.

"No," I whispered back. And as clear as I remembered being naked and hugging my naked friend, I remembered feeling fear. I also remembered from where I was, underneath the bed looking toward the back corner of the room, I saw two boots. They were the boots of an adult. And, just like that, I remember realizing I wasn't hugging my friend out of childlike curiosity. I was holding onto her for dear life. Something had happened. And that something didn't have anything to do with her and had everything to do with whomever's feet were at the end of that bed. At this point in the exercise we were only a couple of minutes in, but I couldn't take it anymore. I leapt up from my chair and rushed out of the room. Nancy followed me.

"Talk to me, Carlos," she said. I was weeping and couldn't catch my breath. She grabbed my hand and simply held it. I was in full-blown panic mode. Again. *What and where had this memory come from? Was I making it up?* I couldn't have been making it up. It was so real. It was so incredibly real. I could touch it. I could taste it. I knew it was real. I knew I was underneath that bed absolutely terrified, and so was my friend. I knew now that my lips weren't chapped because of my friend. I knew that something horrible had happened, but I couldn't remember anything else.

"Carlos, can you talk to me now?" I awakened from my mind warp, and I told Nancy everything that had just come out in my exercise. I told her I didn't know if I had made it up or if it was real. I told her I didn't know where it came from. I'd never had this memory before.

"Carlos. You didn't make this up. And I can tell you where it came from. It came from finally being safe enough to remember it—from finally being at a safe place. When you were staring into Tom's eyes, he never looked away. He gave you that safety. It's gonna be okay. Let's stay right there, under that bed. With five-year-old Carlos. Let's talk to him for a minute and let him know that it's going to be okay."

So we did.

I'd love to tell you that after five minutes and that

conversation with Nancy, I got to the bottom of whose feet those were and what happened, but, the truth is that I still haven't completely uncovered that memory. I keep chipping away at it with prayer, conversations, and therapy. A little more is exposed every time I open it up, but God hasn't revealed to me the full story behind that memory. Half of me is frustrated by that, but the other half of me is grateful because I got to a place where I felt shame. And for the longest time, I had no idea why I felt so shameful. For the longest time, I had no idea why I could not avoid stomping all over my blessings. I couldn't just relish the good things that came into my life. I inevitably did something to ruin them. And in this moment, in this safety, I think I found out why.

We must get back to the place where our spider was birthed. It may take some work, but it's so worth it! What can get you there? A memory? A song? A conversation? Maybe you don't want to go there. Maybe you have managed to claw your way out of the darkness, with your own strength, and you have managed to get to place of a nice, safe, happy existence, so why in the world would you want to go to a place that makes you remember all that pain? Let me tell you why. The freedom you have achieved for yourself, with your own strength, is only temporary freedom. It's cobweb-cleaning freedom. But the spider is still alive and well. Yet we don't have to be afraid of the darkness, because when we bring God to those dark places, the places are no longer dark. Psalm 139:11–12 (NLT) says:

> I could ask the darkness to hide me and the light
> around me to become night—but even in darkness
> I cannot hide from you. To you the night shines

as bright as day. Darkness and light are the same to you.

It's right there. God is LIGHT. And He is there in the darkness. We don't need to be scared of going back to those dark places.

Of course, you may be wondering what to do if you aren't scared but have no idea where to begin looking. Well, a few verses later, David tells us,

> Search me, O God, and know my heart;
>> test me and know my anxious thoughts.
> Point out anything in me that offends you,
>> and lead me along the path of everlasting life.
>
> PSALM 139:23-24 NLT

We get to ask God to point out things, to reveal things to us. And He will!

We will get to a place later in my story where I'll give you some words. Some words to throw up toward God if you can't seem to find them on your own. So keep with me! I know it's not the sweet and savory stuff we are sitting in right now, but trust me when I say it will be worth it.

What Will You Do with What You Discover When You Find Where Your Spider Was Born?

There is a whole lot of truth lying around, waiting for us at that spot where our spider was born. It isn't always a welcome sight, though. In fact, I think it's safe to say that none of us will enjoy encountering what we find there. That's the uncomfortable fact of this situation. I mean, we don't hide from or try to forget the good stuff after all. You are going to have to do some not-so-pleasant work here, but once you do, that spider won't be able to elude you any longer.

- Can you muster the courage to take an honest look at where your spider was born?
- Will you commit to sticking with it and not running away even when it gets tough?

✹

PRAYER

When my eyes opened the next morning, they didn't move left or right. They just stared straight up. The ceiling fan above my bed was strangely therapeutic. As I watched it go around and around I recollected my week so far. I'd left my family for a week. I'd given up my connection to the outside world (my phone). I'd accidentally stopped believing in God. I had discovered a memory of something horrible happening to me when I was just a little boy. At this rate, by the end of the week I would be a thousand times worse off than when I showed up. This was not going as I had anticipated. My thought was that by day four I would be four times better of a human being than I was when I showed up, but I felt like I was going backward. Things were hurting in places in my soul that I hadn't even known existed. This wasn't what I signed up for.

So after laying there for fifteen minutes, I thought, *God, if there is still one, we need to talk.* I walked over to my suitcase and pulled out my running shoes. The shoes that I pack on every trip with the intention of using them, but they never make it out of the bag. That day, they were going to be more therapy than I knew at that moment. I walked out of the cabin and hit the pavement with a pace normally reserved for a seventeen-year-old cross-country runner, not a forty-year-old out-of-shape dad. But something inside of me was raging and I needed to get it out.

As I came up the bluff and saw the scene of the crime from earlier that week, the labyrinth, I started yelling. I started yelling at God. Literally. Yelling. As my volume grew louder, so did my pace. Before I knew it, I was at the bottom of a hill by a creek and completely out of breath and strength. I stopped yelling and moving. I found a tree and sat down.

And then I just started sobbing. Like the sobbing that should be reserved for funerals. And you know what? At the time, I kind of felt like it was a funeral. A funeral of every-thing I believed. But if I didn't believe anymore, then why was I screaming at God? Why was I praying? It's like there was, at the core of who I was, a glimmer of hope.

This prayer didn't look or feel like any sort of prayer I was used to. But at the core, that's what it was. A prayer.

We are about to dive into a section of the book that covers prayer. I'm going to talk about it *a lot*. And if you are anything like me, you will want to completely skip it and just get to the stuff that you don't have to fold into a pack-age and mail to a great big God in the sky. At least that is how I used to view prayer. It was a crap shoot. Some prayers worked. Most prayers didn't. It's not a secret; it's *obvious*. So before you start making agreements about prayer based on your experience with prayer, go with me for a minute.

This prayer thing. I absolutely, inexplicably, tragically

suck at it. I have never even remotely understood the potential in it or the significance of it.

When we are children, or at least when I was a kid, I was taught to pray for my food.

I think it went something like this:

God is great; God is good. Let us thank Him for our food. Ahhhhhhh-men.

Yup. Up until my teens, this was about as far as I got.

Not because I didn't want to go deeper with God; I think it's because all I was learning in the church was that relationship and communication with God primarily took place before meals, and maybe, if you were superspiritual, for fifteen minutes in the morning for your "quiet time."

That's what the youth group I grew up in called it: "Time Alone with God," or TAWG for short.

"Hey, man. How was your TAWG this morning?" we would riff on each other in youth group.

I would always lie and say something back like, "Oh, man. It was incredible. God really spoke to me."

TAWG? I'm hereby renaming it BOOM—Bring Out Our Master.

"Hey, man. How was your BOOM this morning?"

See. It *already* makes me want to give it a shot.

Truthfully, I don't think I had ever heard God speak to me in the seventeen years I'd had on earth to that point. And if He had spoken to me, why in the world would He choose the fifteen minutes in my bedroom at 7:00 a.m. on a Monday morning while I stared blankly into the student devotional I was reading about not lusting?

In the Bible, God spoke to people through angels, burning bushes, and visions of dragons. Okay, maybe not dragons, but it was always epic. And, somehow, I was supposed to be convinced that God speaks in a quiet time. I wasn't buying it. And I never did.

Cue college.

Here, people were beginning to get really serious about this whole prayer thing. At the small liberal arts school I attended, all the hippie students would gather around in circles at the front door of Frost Chapel and sing songs together. It was called Prayer and Praise. I loved Prayer and Praise. I even bought a guitar to strum along. The prayers were always filled with concern for roommates "far from God" and prayers for the healing of sickness. "Dear God, Please, I beg, Amen." Their prayers were filled with that kind of stuff. But I'd say these nights were about five minutes of prayer and sixty minutes of singing. All the pretty girls were there, so I got really good at this sort of prayer.

I don't think I ever even heard if any of these "prayers" were answered. We definitely did not have Prayer and Praise check-ins. It was simply missile launch prayers into the sky, and we hoped they would hit their target.

I'm thinking that the distance between the prayer I prayed as a preschooler for my food and these Prayer and Praise missiles was about two inches. It's easy to read this as "Carlos is disrespecting prayer. God hears all of our prayers!" I don't mean to disrespect anyone else's prayers, but I'm not sure I ever grew deeper in my faith or closer to God through this type of prayer. It was something that felt so very . . . ordinary.

Venturing into adulthood prayer didn't get much deeper. But I did become acutely aware that it was supposed to be. At the church where I was on staff, there was a woman named Sue. She was about twenty-five years older than the rest of us. Every time she would come around me, I would feel peace like no other. You know those types of people, right? They just exude peace. When she would look me in the eye, she would pierce straight to my soul.

Sue served as our "Prayer Minister." The first time I heard her pray, it was as if somebody placed an oxygen mask on me. I could breathe. It was mind blowing.

There was something different about her when she prayed. I can only describe it as *real*.

When she would pray for me, I felt the world stop. It was like nothing I had experienced before. It wasn't a listing of needs. It was a conversation with God, almost as if she could actually hear Him responding.

I remember wanting to be able to pray like that, desiring communion with God like that. I also remember believing that there was no way I could ever pull that off. As jacked up as my faith was, I could barely walk a straight line into church, much less pray the paint off the walls. There's that "fraud" lie again. Sigh.

At least I had Sue. At least I could get her to pray for me whenever I needed. But how could I get my prayer life to look like hers?

A tattoo! I could get a huge tattoo on my forearm that said "PRAY."

Only I wouldn't get it in English, because the last thing I wanted was for someone to know that I had *pray* on my arm, so I got it in Korean.

Gidohada. To pray.

(I went to Korean churches to ask what the symbols I was going to get tattooed on my arm meant. They all said, "To pray.")

The day I got my tattoo, I ran into one of my Korean friends. He was with his mom.

She looked at my arm and started laughing.

"What? What's so funny?" I asked.

She said something in Korean to my friend.

"She wants to know why you have that on your arm," he replied.

"Um. Because it's a spiritual discipline I want to grow in," I answered.

He said something in Korean to his mom, and she said something back.

"She wants to know what spiritual discipline 'to squat' is."

I froze. Every ounce of brown pigmentation in my Panamanian body left me in that moment. I am sure I turned pale. I could not believe this. *Did I really tattoo "to squat" on my* . . .

"We're messing with you, man. I told her to mess with you!"

Nonetheless, I now was the proud owner of a tattoo that (in theory) would help me pray every day for the rest of my life. Or squat. Whatever. I felt so spiritual!

And guess how many days I prayed in the days and weeks following. *Zero.*

The only time I really prayed for anything was when I needed something *major* in my life. At those times, I would turn on the "I Believe in Prayer" switch. Honestly, I did believe. I prayed holes in the knees of my jeans when I suffered my anxiety attack. I prayed so hard when we went to adopt our son, Losiah. I prayed morning, noon, and night for my uncle Roger when he was diagnosed with cancer. With the massive things in life, *everyone* believes in prayer.

So, at our root, all of mankind wants to believe it is possible to get ahold of our God and ask Him for help. But could there be more? Could our God actually have given us the Holy Spirit that allows us to commune with Him not only in crisis and when we need something, but to walk and talk with us daily, in the everyday moments of life? Could the prayer life my friend Sue has be available to us all? Could we *really* and *truly* have direct access to God not only to help us, but to talk with us, laugh with us, cry with us, and *be* with us?

In order to get at the crux of this question, I had to ask myself one, simple question: If I believe in the God of the impossible, then why do I not believe in the God of the possible?

Can't He be the God of the normal—who can, if we ask, tell us where we need to go to lunch, exactly where we need to move, how much money we need to budget for movies next month, and where the heart of our spider is and exactly how to kill it?

Yes. This is our God. This is the God I read about in Scripture. This is the God who is ready to go into battle with us.

But how? How can we talk to God like this? How can we hear from God like this? How can we have this weapon of prayer at our disposal and use it to get to the root of our sin and away from the cobwebs?

I've got the answer. Are you ready? Do you have your Moleskine with empty pages and a new pen ready to furiously write down the pages of instructions I'm about to give you? Okay, here it is: Just . . . begin.

Just gaze at Him. Just look at Him. Right now. Look at Him. "Where do I look, Carlos?" Good question. Look toward the place you have felt Him before. Was it a verse that gave you a sudden breath? Was it in the mountains where you saw the vastness of His creation? Was it on a date with your spouse where He showed you how much He cares for you? Go to that place and stare at Him for a bit.

A few years ago, my family and I were on one of our many road trips across the country. We had stopped at a hotel to spend the night. It was a hole-in-the-wall hotel with two double beds. As you can guess, five humans and two double beds meant we were gonna share. Heather, Losiah, and I shared a bed together.

I woke up the next morning to Losiah sticking his finger in my right nostril. I didn't open my eyes because I was intrigued as to his intentions. He was doing it very lightly, trying not to wake me. His tracing finger moved to my eyelids, rubbing them lightly. He then traced his finger down to my lips. He plucked them like someone would a bass guitar. I heard a giggle. Then his tiny finger traced its way to my ears. My ears are really ticklish, so it took all I had to not burst out laughing. But I was intrigued, so I hung in there. And then yes, he traced his way around the maze in my earlobe like the race car driver he dreamt of becoming, all the while making those race car sounds: "Vrrroooom, eeeerrrrrrkkkkkkkkk, pckwshhhhhhhh!"

His hand then slowly traced its way to my chest. It stopped there, flat against it. I could feel him staring at me while feeling my heartbeat. His wispy hair then landed on my chest and I felt his breathing slow down. It wasn't long before he was back asleep after searching every crease of his father's face. I shed a tear of joy in that moment that he just wanted to see my face and know it so deeply.

I shed another that I had not done that with my Father in a long time—maybe not ever—just staring at His face with no more intention than wanting to know His face better. And that is where I want you to start.

After you get that down for a few days, you can start the conversation part of this by talking to God and asking Him some stuff.

I'm serious. Now you can return your empty Moleskine to Barnes and Noble, because it's not gonna take a seminary degree to walk and talk with God.

You've got this. Now, let's take a step a little deeper.

In a conversation, there are two people talking. One has to *not* be talking while the other one is talking. It is scientifically proven that you cannot hear someone else talking while you are talking. As far as I can tell, we are really good at talking to (or maybe at) God.

But let's look at the other side of the conversation. How are we supposed to hear? The Bible puts it pretty clearly: "There is so much more I want to tell you, but you can't bear it now. When the Spirit of truth comes, he will guide you into all truth. He will not speak on his own but will tell you what he has heard. He will tell you about the future" (John 16:12–13 NLT). This is meant to be normal! To hear from God!

And here, "Anyone who belongs to God listens gladly to the words of God" (John 8:47 NLT).

Come with me back to the bottom of the hill during my run. While I was sitting against that tree next to the creek, I had declared some pretty powerful things. I had yelled them. I was sitting there, out of breath, waiting. Waiting for what? Waiting for God to speak. At the very least He should have sent a lightning bolt down from the heavens to scare the crap out of me. But no. He didn't. Instead I saw two butterflies. Playing with each other and enjoying their butterfly day. I actually got annoyed. *Answer me, God!* I yelled. Silence.

I wanted an answer from God, but I had not asked a question.

Try Having a Conversation with God (as Opposed to Giving a Speech to God)

I learned something about that. I needed to actually open up a conversation with God and not just talk at Him. It took some time, but I got there. I now have a journal where my wife has written a daily prayer that we pray every day. It centers our hearts with the heart of God. Then I use the pages of the journal to write down where the Lord is taking me. There are many daily prayers out there—ones that align us to the voice of God throughout the day. Heather and I basically have taken a piece from here and there in order to get to something that works for us. Remember, this is a conversation between you and God, so you can manipulate our idea in ways that work for where you are. But in its essence, beginning your day with something that simply opens you up to hearing from God will help you in your conversation with the Lord during your day.

If you are comfortable trying to start a conversation with God on your own, by all means, dive in and start communicating! But, if you think you need some help getting things rolling, try this prayer and see where things go.

———————

Dear Lord, I come to You to be renewed in You right now. I know this isn't magic. But I know this is true. That You are absolutely listening to me at this moment. I'm coming to You with some unbelief right now. I pray that You take my unbelief and change it. I ask You simply, could You show me something today that tells me how much I mean to You? Will You show me today something that declares Your love to me? And when You show me, will You open my eyes that I may see and receive it? I will walk with You today and keep my eyes open. In the name of Jesus I pray, amen.

———————

INTERLUDE

Let's go back in time a bit to my initial panic attacks. Counseling, medication, diet, exercise, and lots of prayer helped me claw my way out of the hole called despair that I was in for a few months after it started. I worked *hard* to get out of that spot. I refused to go down without a fight.

And there was fruit coming from my work. Within a few months, I was back leading worship. Within a few years, I was leading the creative process at one of the largest churches in the country. And ten years after I was stricken with anxiety, I was signed to the biggest worship record label in the world alongside Hillsong United, Israel Houghton, and Paul Baloche. I was standing on stages in front of 40,000 people singing my songs, and they were singing them back.

If you were watching my social media reports, you figured things were incredible. I had a gorgeous wife and beautiful kids. I was living on tour buses and traveling all over the world. The cobwebs were gone! Well, at least the ones anyone could see.

The desire in my heart to be a fully devoted follower of Christ was there. I *wanted* to be a better husband. I *wanted* to be a fully present dad. I *wanted* to believe the words I was singing as I stood in front of thousands of people every week declaring the greatness of our God. But pure desire wasn't pulling it off. It was such a messy and broken season of faith and trials.

I love Paul when he tells us to consider our trials not only to be joy, but *great* joy: "Consider it a great joy, my brothers, whenever you experience various trials, knowing that the testing of your faith produces endurance" (James 1:2–3 CSB).

Really? Our trials are supposed to be a *great* joy? Man, I have a long way to go in my spiritual walk. But I want you to know that it is okay to wrestle like this. It is okay to wrestle with your faith. Look at where we are in my OnSite story: I was expecting to waltz with my faith, not to wrestle with it.

But there I was, exhausted and out of breath at the bottom of a hill because the wrestling had gotten *so intense*. My friends, please don't give up because you are now wrestling. You see, that's the work. That is the work that some of you are going to have to do in order to get to your spiders. For some of you, you may already be there. You may already be face-to-face with your spider. But it took work. And it is going to take more work.

Even in the midst of the wrestling match, there was some incredible learning going on. I wasn't going to go down without a fight, and fight I did. Press on I did. Roll up my sleeves I did. I went *all* in.

One of my favorite times of the day at OnSite was our large group meetings. They happened after breakfast and before small group time. As I mentioned before, we would all gather together and Bill would deliver some incredible nuggets as to why we were dealing with the cobwebs we were dealing with.

Bill called them "medicators." One afternoon he talked about codependency.

Codependency is the excessive emotional or psychological reliance on a partner, typically a partner who requires support due to an illness or addiction.

I mentally checked out. If there was one thing that I knew I did not have a problem with, it was codependency. Nope. Not me. Next issue please . . . But right smack-dab in the middle of Bill's lesson on codependency, he said something that sent a shiver up my spine. "Some of you are addicted to relationships. Some of you are relationship addicts. The high that your body naturally releases when a new person finds you interesting or attractive, that high . . . it's your drug and just as addicting as any other drug."

You know that feeling you get when you are cruising down the freeway at 80 mph in a 70 mph zone without another car in sight and no worries in the world, and you suddenly pass a cop car hidden in the bushes? You know *that* feeling? The feeling of your blood suddenly freezing in your veins? Yeah. That's what I felt when Bill described this relationship addict. That was me on so many levels. Bill went on to explain that this isn't just promiscuous relationships. This can work in any relationship. Some of it is absolutely normal. But for some of us in the room, it is a dangerous addiction that can result in the loss of everything we hold dear to us. All for a fix. While he was talking, all I could think about was my life just a year prior. A year that I finally could put words around. For years I had been a relationship addict, taking a hit whenever I could. And so when Bill was done with that morning's lesson, I sprinted up to him.

"Bill, I think that's me! IS it me?"

"I don't know, but if you think this looks like something you may struggle with, my guess is that you are onto something," Bill replied.

Man, not only do I know that I rub crap on my blessings, but now I'm also a *relationship addict*! Lord, have mercy on my therapy bills.

But it's the work that needs to be done! It's the work that needs to happen in your story before you can get to where you meet your spider face-to-face. Unpack it. You can unpack it in a therapist's office, or you can unpack it with your best friends. You can unpack it in a blog post. It doesn't matter the method of unpacking; it just matters that you do the work and unpack it. And that is where we are heading—to a part of my story that I've never publicly unpacked. But a part of the story that, when finally unpacked, was the key to the door that led me straight to my spider.

So if you take anything from the words in this chapter, please let it be this: Whether you are almost to your spider, have killed your spider, or are galaxies away from your spider, keep pressing on. Keep seeking God. Just as many of you may feel He is unreachable as you read this chapter, take comfort in the assurance that He is right here with you. He never left. The incredible thing about our God is that our resistance has nothing to do with His residence in our lives. He is here, friends. And He is going to be the strength we need to move one step closer to killing the spider.

Are You Willing to Show up Broken and Ready?

Maybe you're like me and you procrastinate and find every excuse under the sun to keep from doing the uncomfortable or unpleasant parts of life. But what good is waiting until we are no longer broken to start healing?

- What can you do to release your expectations of how a relationship with God is supposed to look?
- What is holding you back from trying to pray? How can you move past that and take those first steps toward God?

ALL IS LOST

Let's put it all on the table. I had reached a point in my life journey where I was caught up in *lots* of cobwebs. Many of them I'd cleaned up, some more aggressively than others. But I was really good at cleaning them.

Alcohol. Approval addiction. Pornography. They never felt too sinister to me because I'd let them accumulate for a few weeks, then I'd clean them out for months at a time. After having repeated the process too many times, though, I found that the cobwebs were coming back a little bigger and a little stronger. The cobweb of alcohol went from having a drink to "taking the edge off" to drinking to forget the reality of life I was in. The cobweb of approval addiction went from always apologizing even if I wasn't wrong to compromising my morals just for a compliment. The cobweb of pornography went from finding intimacy in a make-believe scene being portrayed on my laptop to a real-life emotional involvement playing out on my phone. But I'd keep cleaning up after myself, trying to keep these cobwebs a secret.

When it all fell apart, truth be told, the details for me

aren't that much different from when things fell apart for you. The characters and the setting may be different, but the results are the same—total and complete devastation. And, to be honest, the specific cobweb that you end up getting tangled in enough that you can no longer escape doesn't even matter. It could have been any of them. I know I tended to focus on what happened right before I hit rock bottom and point to that as the cause for everything coming apart. If I could avoid doing that again, it'd be great. But the truth is, that was just the proverbial straw that broke the camel's back. To figure out what happened, why it happened, and how to fix it requires going way back, way before rock bottom. It means going beyond the surface cleaning that got the cobwebs you could see to the ones that hide in less conspicuous places.

Kenny, one of my counselors told me once, "Carlos, when most marriages fail, people want to look at the final play of the game, just like a football game. The headline in the paper will say that the receiver lost the game—that he dropped the last pass in the end zone for his team and lost the game. That is what the papers are gonna write the next morning. But you know what? That last play is seldom what lost the game. The game was lost in the third quarter when the lineman missed that block, and it was lost in the second quarter when the coach forgot to call that time-out and regroup his players. The game was lost before it even began because there was not nearly enough attention paid to the opponent because they seemed like such an easy victory. The game is never lost on the last play. That is normally just the loudest play, and it's always gonna be what people want to pay attention to. But if you want to fix your marriage, we aren't gonna look at the last play because by that point you were long gone anyway. We are gonna have to study all the game film."

Maybe Kenny had unfulfilled aspirations of becoming a football coach. I don't know. But I'm glad he put it that way because it made total sense to me. And yes, as you may have guessed by reading what Kenny said to me, my marriage most definitely fell apart.

The morning after my life imploded, I was delivered a handwritten letter from Heather. It was six pages long and, as I read it, it became clear that life as I knew it was over. But I also knew that she was sitting in the presence of God, because it was a "Dear John" letter and a love letter all wrapped up in one. It started with:

> *Dear Carlos,*
>
> *It's strange thinking that this will be the last love letter I will ever write with that name on it, but the thought of it all coming to an end made me want to write you a love letter. Not because I'm busting with love for you, but because I do love the Carlos I once knew. You are so full of kindness, you are a great father, and we got the chance to do so many amazing things together. Thank you for allowing me to raise my babies and for always saying yes to my crazy ideas . . .*

It went on to tell me that she would never say a bad word about me in front of the kids and that she would do her best to co-parent with me in a way that was reflective of God. It also went on to confirm the fact that the relationship was over and she was moving on, but that she prayed for the best for me.

I'll never forget the feeling of nausea that washed over me as I got to the end of the letter. *It was over.* As I ran to the toilet to empty the remaining contents of my stomach, I could not imagine a scenario in a hundred years where I might get my family back. But the incredible thing about my imagination is that it's not God's imagination. Our imaginations are incredibly limited, but God's plan is so much greater.

The devil is an opportunist, and the darkest of hours and the loneliest of times is when he is going to come in and start telling lies for you to make agreements with. And it's here, when you are most vulnerable, that the enemy comes diving in like a vulture to prey on your wounded heart. I certainly was no different. For a solid month, I barely ate. I was staying with a family that was not mine, only seeing my kids every other day. I had zero communication with Heather. She was done. As well she should have been.

From what I could gather from friends, Heather seemed better than she had ever been. I mean, she was rid of this massive weight that had been dragging her down. How could she not be feeling better? When I would go in to talk to Kenny, I would ask about Heather because he was counseling both of us. He would shoot me a painful and uncomfortable look of, "It's over bro," before quickly changing the subject back to my healing.

And then one day he gave me some advice that shined a light into a crack of hope I never would have seen without it. He said, "Carlos, you keep spilling to me how absolutely awful you are. You keep texting Heather asking for forgiveness over and over again. You keep telling yourself that you are a worthless piece of dirt. Listen. It's time to start looking at truth. It's time to start speaking truth. That marriage is over. Stop trying to get it back. It's time to start focusing on God's truth. I don't want you texting Heather anymore. If you feel you must reach out to her, you can send her one truth every few days—share something you've learned about God's truth. That's it. But you have to start filling your heart with truth." And so I did.

I stopped trying to get my family back and started trying to get my soul back. I sent Heather one truth a day for months. I did not know until years later that she never read any of them. She deleted them all. But you know what? I've realized that, although I thought they were for her, they weren't. They were for me. I needed to start living in the truth of who God is. I needed to start bathing in the truth of who I was in God's eyes. The circumstances I was in were all on me.

Kenny was so right. Yes, I had lost my wife. I had lost my family. I was living in a friend's spare bedroom. My ministry was over. All that was lost. Everything was gone—everything but God.

Listen, as dire as that sounds, when things are bleakest is when God has the most room to work. We don't need to spend a lot of time on how the Israelites kept messing up over and over. God had promised the Israelites the land of Canaan, so Moses sent spies to check out the land. They came back saying, "Yup. It's incredible. But we ain't got the manpower to pull off this upset. If we try, we die." And so all the people lost heart because of the report of a few spies. Scripture says, "Our brothers have made us lose heart" (Deuteronomy 1:28 CSB). Out of the mouth of men, God's promises were destroyed.

But there were two spies who had not lost heart. They reminded the people that God promised, and therefore He would provide. And many times He provides in ways we would LEAST expect His provision. In this case, it was from the heart of a prostitute named Rahab. The land of Canaan was given to the Israelites through the heart and hands of a prostitute. Sometimes we need to take our eyes off of the steeple and place them on the people in order to watch God provide. Rahab risked her life and the life of her family in order to let these two spies into the walls of Jericho. She told a blatant and outright lie to the king's men, all to protect these spies who she knew would destroy her city. But she had heard the stories of their God and she believed in their God. That gave her strength. And God's people, because of her actions, were able to take the city of Jericho.

How many times do we lose heart *after* God has promised us the land of milk and honey? People in our lives may even be trying to help you out of your despair.

In the middle of all this madness, in the thickness of my despair, someone told me that they hoped I felt the wrath of pain for my sins, because that pain would remind me of how bad it hurt and to never stray from God's plan again. I wept when I heard this. It sounded right. I was almost convinced that God had this plan set up for me—that His plan was pain as punishment. I just didn't know how long. But then I related this idea to another friend, one I trusted and admired. This friend spoke words I knew to be true: "It's God's kindness that leads to repentance, not God's wrath. God already died for your sins. You don't have to climb back on that cross for Him."

Truth. You must find the truth. You must find those

willing to tell you that truth. The Israelites were ready to give up, but two spies out of the ten reminded the people that God promised and He would deliver! Who will remind *you* of God's incredible promises and truth? This is a moment of decision for many of you, not a moment of relegation. This is a moment of rescue.

For four excruciating months, I lived apart from my wife and kids. Through nothing I did, nor due to any prodding on her friends' part—who rightfully thought I did not deserve another chance—Heather was led by the Spirit to sit with me. That's it. Just sit with me. So we sat on a park bench in Sylvan Park in Nashville. I'll never forget that meeting. She was *so* content without me.

By this point in our trial, I had already resigned myself to the fact that I was not getting my wife back. So I did not show up with a speech prepared to win her back. Instead, I had accepted the reality that if I were ever to get my family back, it was going to have to come together by the hand of God alone. I was, however, going to tell her the truth of where I was. And I did. And she listened. And there was absolutely *zero* wooing from me. She could smell that wooing stuff from a mile away. She had been married to me for years after all. No, I just told her the truth. I remember using my cup from Jack in the Box as an illustration. I told her if that cup was Mount Everest, I was sitting at the bottom of it, and looking all the way up to the top was terrifying—the top being having my life back together—but I was gonna get there, even if it had to be my life's work. And then she said something that was truly a gift, perhaps a sort of preface to *Kill the Spider,* if you will. "I think you are right. That last straw—the one that broke this whole thing up—I'm glad you aren't just trying to fix that. Because that would be similar to you getting in a car wreck and then putting a Band-Aid on, trying to fix a cut on your finger when there is internal bleeding."

There it was again: truth. I was being repaired by the best surgeon in the universe. He was fixing my internal bleeding. And then she said this: "I'm not going to give you a second chance, Carlos. I'm not. I'm not going to go back to that marriage. That marriage is over. There is no second chance at it. But I do see Christ impacting you in ways I never have before. Let's talk again tomorrow. More about God. Not about us." And so we did. And we did again. And again. And before you knew it, we were building a new relationship—one that was being built on Christ alone.

Four months after I moved out, I moved back in. It was a surreal experience. I had removed any and all expectations of ever living with my family again. But, again, the fantastic thing about God is that we don't rely on our own plans. The kids had also removed any expectations of what the future would hold. The only promises we made to them at the beginning of all the madness were that Mom was going to be okay. Dad was going to be okay. And they were going to be okay. I had turned that advice into a song and would sing it to them every time I would drop them back off at the house. We would sing it together. "Momma's gonna be okay. Daddy's gonna be okay. I'm gonna be okay. We're all gonna be okay!" When I turned that into a song, I didn't know what okay meant. I didn't know what that would look like. But I did have enough faith in God, just barely, but enough to know that I would survive it. I think it's because even in the worst moment, the absolute bottom, God showed up.

Here's what you need to understand: My spider wasn't killed when I moved back in. I was simply on my way to finding it. Heather and I were determined not to try to "fix" our marriage. We knew that wouldn't work. It's been an incredibly difficult journey to get to this place, but so worth it. I think I saw it initially as God releasing my family from me. But soon enough I saw it as God rescuing me *for* my family. This was the beginning of the acceleration toward my healing.

I debated long and hard about whether to write this chapter. It was such a devastating time, and I have not gone into detail about the cobweb because, at the end, the name of the cobweb isn't important. Just know that rock bottom is out there, and if you are already there, rescue will come if you let it. When you are utterly in despair, here are some truths:

Truth #1: God *has not* abandoned you. If anything, you are now at a place where you will hear Him louder than ever if you slow down, stop talking, and listen. Know that He is there.

Psalm 139:1–12 (ESV) tells us how God is so there that He knows everything about us.

> O LORD, you have searched me and known me!
> You know when I sit down and when I rise up;
>> you discern my thoughts from afar.
> You search out my path and my lying down
>> and are acquainted with all my ways.
> Even before a word is on my tongue,
>> behold, O LORD, you know it altogether.
> You hem me in, behind and before,

and lay your hand upon me.
Such knowledge is too wonderful for me;
    it is high; I cannot attain it.

Where shall I go from your Spirit?
    Or where shall I flee from your presence?
If I ascend to heaven, you are there!
    If I make my bed in Sheol, you are there!
If I take the wings of the morning
    and dwell in the uttermost parts of the sea,
even there your hand shall lead me,
    and your right hand shall hold me.
If I say, "Surely the darkness shall cover me,
    and the light about me be night,"
even the darkness is not dark to you;
    the night is bright as the day,
    for darkness is as light with you.

Did you see that? Even the darkness isn't darkness to Him. That light is gonna change everything. No matter who you are and what you have done, God is right there, eager for your heart. *Eager* for your heart. He is right there waiting and wanting.

As you begin to walk in step with Him, you will begin to see clearly who God *is* and who God is *not*—which leads us to this next truth.

Truth #2: As you excavate your days, hold on to God's truths and discard Satan's lies. It will be easy to believe the lies in these moments. Shame, guilt, and self-reproach convince you that you're a screw-up, an idiot. You deserve this. You are alone. Things will never change. You are unlovable.

The enemy is an opportunist and will come streaking

into these moments of destruction. Thankfully, I surrounded myself with people who would help me break these lies. And even if you don't have a team of truth tellers in your life, *you* know. Our God is not a God of shame. He is not a God of guilt. God is not going to shame or guilt you back to Him. So as these feelings begin to rise, defeat them with truth. You are a child of the King. No matter how dark or hideous your sin is, there is mercy, grace, and redemption coming. Yours is a story of radical grace, not a story of ridicule and pain.

One step at a time. Stand up. Take a deep breath. Gaze up. Glance down. It's time to walk up to the spider. It's time to stare at the spider. It's time to kill the spider.

What Can You Silence in Your Busy Life to Increase the Decibel Level of the Voice of God?

It is so easy for us to get too busy living life to hear God and so broken by the cycle of wounding that His voice is drowned out by negative messages. He has not left our side even though we might feel horribly alone, but we may need to be still enough to find Him again.

- When was the last time you sat still and quiet enough to give God a chance to make His presence known?
- What are you telling yourself, or letting the enemy tell you, that contradicts what God would say if you were listening to Him?
- How can you make time in your day, every day, to stop long enough for God to penetrate all the other noise and tell you what you need to hear?

GOD WANTS TO GIVE US DISNEY WORLD

The day came when it was my turn to share my experiential family portrait. Remember Sharon? *Yeah.* I thought, *I think I'll be okay during this one. After all, I have loving parents, who are still together, who love Jesus and love me and have always provided everything I have ever needed. This will take about two minutes, then we can move on to the people in our group who were wounded by their parents as a child.* This was my mindset going into small group that morning.

"Okay, Carlos," Nancy began. "It's your turn. Can you explain your family to us and then pick a few people from the group to play your family?"

"If I could just teleport the Cleavers into the room right now, I would. My childhood was majestic. This should go by fast, amigos," I declared.

I went on to select John as my dad. I looked at Sharon and smiled poetically. I hope she didn't think she was gonna get out of this one after she made me be her grand-father. She started moving toward me before I even opened my mouth to ask. Sharon would be my mom.

There was a guy in my group named Ben. He was the class clown and could turn any moment when it felt like the walls were caving into the room and not only keep them from falling, but have us laughing our heads off. Nancy had to put him in time-out a few times. Not actual time-out, but that *look*. That look she would give you when you were not being involved with someone else's story. That look. It was time-out enough. Ben would be me.

I arranged all of us in the center of the room. I had us all hold hands. Because *look* at us! *We* are incredible and full of love and support! Take *that*, everyone with childhood issues!

We were the Whittaker Circle of Life. We were mak-ing the *Lion King* jealous. We were the family at the end of every Disney movie. Together and secure.

"Can you explain to us what you have created here?" asked Nancy.

"Sure. This is my dad, this is my mom, and this is me. We are all holding hands, and we are all there for each other. This is it. It was simple. It was perfect." I replied. I was ready for her to let us all sit back down so the next person could go.

"Were your parents first generation immigrants into this country?" she asked.

I have mentioned already how Nancy is a wiz in the ther-apy department, but I had no idea she was also a *prophet*.

"Um. *Wow*. How in the world did you know that?" I answered.

"This is very similar to how children of first generation immigrants set up their family portrait."

What? Holding hands in a circle? That didn't seem very "immigrant" to me. Until I looked at the circle again. Wait.

"You are all facing out, Carlos. Nobody is facing each other." Nancy spoke softly this time. As if to let the gravity of what I had just built with my groupmates sink in.

"I don't know why I have our backs facing each other. That's not what I meant. Let me—"

"Nope," Nancy continued. "This is what you have created and this is what it is. This isn't bad. This doesn't mean you guys never looked at each other. This just means that your father and mother were having to do five times as much looking out as they were looking in. Protection. Safety. They loved you. Don't worry."

I slowly looked back over the circle of life. The one where I had us all looking out. Something wasn't right about it. Not just the looking out part. Something else.

"I read in your file this morning that you have a brother. Where is he? Where is he in this portrait?"

Titanic anchor to my gut.

"Brian! Can you come here? I don't know what happened. I was so busy thinking about my parents and making sure I didn't have any issues with them that my brother slipped my mind! Can you come stand here—"

"No. You left him out. Let's start there."

And start there we did. In a matter of minutes, I had accidentally painted the upside-down version of my childhood. The version that I didn't even know existed.

Almost like an alternate universe. Like on *Stranger Things*. The show on Netflix. The Upside Down was the darker version of their reality. What I had just modeled with my groupmates was a reality that was not being played in my head.

I had never been close with my brother. I had picked on him and pushed him aside. I had been selfish with my entire being anytime he had been around. As adults, we completely separated. No fighting. Just silence, which is honestly worse than a fight because it made me forget him. It made me completely remove him from my family. We spent some time digging into the obvious issue I had with being an immigrant family. The wounds that I had buried that dealt with being a Hispanic family from East LA moving to the suburbs of the south. Racism hidden in southern sweetness. I was the only kid with brown skin and curly hair in my classes.

It all came tumbling out. We worked for two hours on my story and I found some major points of healing that needed to happen.

Hard conversations. Conversations that I didn't want to have. There is nothing fun about confronting an issue when you don't really know how someone is going to respond. Everyone is telling you that it will make life better. Everyone is telling you that when you have that conversation, when you face that point in your story, healing will come. But it is so much easier to just keep looking away. Life is good. It's moving right along. No need to mess up the cruise control. As I finished my session in that little room made up of my mock family, I remembered something that happened with my kids about a year before.

Not long before my therapist said I should go to OnSite, Heather and I were enjoying me not being an idiot every other day. The kids were enjoying having a dad that wasn't taking selfies to feed his self-esteem every five seconds. We were in what I like to call a "good season" after a time when things were absolutely falling apart. Some of you—you know who you are—were all in with me, scraping the bottom of the barrel of life and at an all-time low like I was. Many of you flipped through that chapter thinking, *Oh, poor Carlos. Thank God I'm nowhere near that place in life.* And thank God for seasons, right? But it's in those good seasons of life when we really should be focusing our spider-killing training. Who trains for a battle while they are immersed in it?

One of my dear friends, Levi Lusko, has an incredible story of pain and promise that illustrates this well. Levi and his incredible family lost one of their own to Heaven. Even though their hope in Heaven was tangible and real, the pain of loss was just as tangible and real. One thing I love that Levi said is this: "Trials reveal foundations; they aren't the ideal time to build them." Well, listen up, all of you "good season"-ers, pain and suffering's off-season is the ideal time for spider killing CrossFit. This is when you buckle down and get ready, because you know that it is just an off-season. Jesus didn't promise a pain-free life. But He did promise He would be with us as we run, skip, limp, crawl, or stumble toward the finish line. Thank God I was done with the whole crawl and stumble thing for the moment. I definitely still had a limp at this point, but I was sporting a solid spiritual cane.

That "good season" is where we were when God showed me how much more He had for me. It's where I was when I went to OnSite—before I even knew what it meant to "kill the spider," but had just purged my life of a bunch of cobwebs. It was good. We were good. But God was still poking me, not letting me get comfortable, telling me, "There is more, my son!" So much more.

The previous summer, we had traveled with the kids for more than 5,000 miles in the back of a Chevy Malibu. (Notice I did not say we rented an RV or a fifteen-passenger van. It wasn't even a humble minivan. No, I said a Chevy Malibu—a car named after one of the most beautiful places on earth. Why in the world would you name a car "Malibu"? That is only begging for disappointment.) Even so, they did it like champions.

I only traveled about 1,500 of those with them, so I had not been pushed as close to lunacy as the wife had. But she assured me they had been amazing, and we were now on the last leg.

We pulled into Orlando via Panama City around 3:30 on Monday morning. I hauled every child like a sack of potatoes slung over my shoulder into Grandma's house and placed them in their sleeping bags.

The first sack of potatoes—Sohaila—had developed some fairly fierce elbows and knees, and it seemed no matter how I arranged this sack of potatoes over my shoulder, one or more of her four body weapons jabbed me in the ribs, neck, or stomach. She basically was a nine-year-old sack of bones.

The second sack—Seanna—was warm and cuddly. This sack clung to me, and I had a hard time putting her down. Even though she was in a deep trance dreaming of who knows what, her body just squeezed tight around my neck and torso as I lifted her out of the car. Heaven.

And then there was the Losiah sack. The kid weighs next to nothing and halfway to the house I had to check my shoulder to make sure he was still there.

There is something about a sleeping child, especially one that you have to drag out of a car that makes them seem like sinless saints, as though there is no way possible they could ever make you regret teaching them to speak or letting them figure out how to walk. It's in these moments that we stare a little longer, pausing a second before walking out of their bedrooms. This was one of those nights—or mornings.

I looked at their tired little bodies on the floor and thought, *I wish I had the money to spoil them with more than just "I love you" and "You're beautiful."*

But then I remembered all the episodes of *The Osbournes* I watched and realized that access to money has nothing to do with growing up sane and loved.

The next morning I could hear Heather and Grandma Sherry trying to figure out what to do with the kids all day. We were only in Orlando for the day, and at the end of this road trip we were broke and beyond tired. The easy thing would have been to send the kids to Grandma's pool while we vegged in front of the TV.

But then it hit me. *Orlando—The Happiest Place on Earth.*

So I tweeted this: "In Orlando for a day. Anyone work at Disney World and want to take my kids for a day so I can actually work?:)"

Three direct messages and two emails later, our entire family had tickets to Disney World.

As I sat alone in the bedroom, I literally cried at the

blessing this Twitter friend had spread over my family. The kids have had a hell of a year, most of it my fault, and today they were going to "The Happiest Place On Earth."

To keep it a surprise for kids, I walked into the kitchen and proudly announced, "Take your bathing suits off. Put back on your shorts and shoes. The plan has changed. We are going to a bounce house." I could see the annoyance on the tweenagers' faces, but Losiah, on the other hand, was naked in two seconds flat. He took off to his suitcase and got dressed in a manner that can only be described as speedy Gonzales and the Tasmanian Devil all wrapped up in one. The kid loves bounce houses.

I don't know why I picked a bounce house. Maybe it's because they didn't exist when I was a kid. We had Sgt. Singer's Pizza Circus, which gave way to Chuck E. Cheese's. But the bounce house was not a thing in the '80s, so I thought it would offer enough excitement to overrule swimming, yet not near the excitement of Disney World so I could still sneak in the surprise. But Losiah . . . I was a tad nervous about his utterly unbridled joy at the current proposition.

We got in the car.

"Siri . . . ," I spoke into my phone.

"Yes, Master?" she replied, because if you don't have Siri call you Master, what good is she?

"What are the directions to Supersonic Bounce House?"

Why did I call it Supersonic Bounce House? These are the sorts of questions that haunt me at night.

"I'm sorry, Master. I can't find any place named Supersonic Bounce House," Siri responded.

I peeked in the rearview mirror and saw my kids' faces.

The girls were annoyed, but Losiah was very into this charade.

"Okay, then, Siri. If you can't give me directions to Supersonic Bounce House . . . give me directions to *Disney World*!"

At this moment, the kids reacted appropriately—two seconds of silence followed by two seconds of talking amongst themselves quietly, "Did he say? Did he say? *Did he say?*"

And then it hit. Screaming and tearing up and going insane. They were losing their minds, so much so that I thought, *Man, what would it take for me to go absolutely bananas like that? What would it take for me to lose my mind like that?* Ah, childlike joy. And then it occurred to me, I was only hearing the girls go nuts. Maybe they were drowning out Losiah's jubilant shouts of praise, so I adjusted the rearview mirror and pointed my eyes at the little man. When I locked him into my gaze he wasn't *nearly* as excited as the girls were. Actually, he didn't look excited at all. Maybe he didn't get it, so I figured I needed to clarify what was happening for him.

"Losiah! We are going to *Disney World*!!! *Woohoo!*"

His straight face slowly started wavering, but wavering in the opposite direction of joy. His tiny bottom lip started trembling. His eyes slowly started filling with liquid. Devastation.

"*Wahhhhh!* I wanted to go to a bounce house! *Wahhhh!* I wanted to go to a *bounce house!*"

Wow. Really?

No. Seriously?

"No, buddy! Did you hear me? *Disney World*! *Disney World*! We are going to see Mickey Mouse!"

Nothing. Nada. He was inconsolable. He obviously wanted to go to a bounce house *way* more than he wanted to go to Disney.

Two hours later, Grandma Sherry texted me a picture of Losiah climbing on a bounce house. He looked like he was having a blast. But I knew the fun he was missing out on.

And then, like a backhand to the side of the face, it hit me. My girls—my tweens—they had been to Disney World before. They had experienced all that "The Happiest Place on Earth" had to offer. They had felt the joy, magic, and wonder that Disney World fills people with. Losiah, on the other hand, had never been to Disney World. He not only had no idea what he was missing, he literally could not care less since he had never experienced it.

He had experienced bounce houses. He knew what awaited him at a bounce house, so he rejected the unknown in his father's offer for Disney World.

Dear Jesus, this must be how You look at us on the daily. This must be how You feel as You are offering us Disney World and all we want is the bounce house.

So often I think I know what I want, but then thirty minutes after jumping all alone in my bounce house, I wish I was with the rest of my family at the Happiest Place On Earth—the place God wanted to take me.

Now don't get all analytical on me. I know there are those of you who would rather be at the bounce house even after knowing what Disney World holds: long lines, 94° heat, and miserable parents growing increasingly impatient with their whiny kids. But you get where I'm going. God has *so much* for us, but sometimes we simply have no clue, or we don't want to do the work (take the risk, extend the trust) that it takes to get to Disney World.

There are cobwebs in the way. There is a spider to kill. And something inside of us knows the freedom and truth that is waiting for us on the other side. This freedom is worth the hunt for the spider. This freedom is worth taking the risk. This freedom is worth the battle that is coming when we will be asked to trust God more than we trust ourselves.

Jeremiah 29:11 is pretty familiar, right? You've seen it on cards, posters, doormats, framed on walls, and maybe even in tattoos.

It is a fantastic verse. It is a hope-giving verse. It is a Disney World verse.

"'For I know the plans I have for you,' declares the LORD, 'plans to prosper you and not to harm you, plans to give you hope and a future.'"

Sign me up. God had Disney World plans for Israel, but if we back up to chapter 28 we see a very different picture. The Israelites had been through a lot. They were God's people with a history of punishment and freedom. But they were up against a new captor—a new spider. This one was named "Babylon." Their newest oppressor.

This is way after Moses had freed them. And there they found themselves again, having dealt with all sorts of horrors at the hands of the Babylonians.

In chapter 28, there was a prophet named Hananiah who told the nation of Israel that they just had to hang tight for two years, and after that time God was gonna free them. The only problem was Hananiah was a false prophet, spitting lies to tickle their ears. This is when the prophet of the Lord, Jeremiah, spoke up. Not only did he tell Israel that, nope, in fact, this was not gonna be the case, he told Hananiah that because he was lying, he would die.

And die he did.

This is the message Jeremiah delivered to Israel from the Lord:

"When seventy years are completed for Babylon, I will come to you and fulfill my good promise to bring you back to this place" (Jeremiah 29:10).

Disney World wasn't coming next week. Disney World wasn't even coming next year. They would have to wait for Disney World for seventy years. *Seventy years!*

Can you imagine the gasps of desperation uttered when they heard that news? I mean, just yesterday they were told they would have to endure being captives in Babylon for only two years. Now it was seventy? And this is news from the God who *loves* them?

So you know what the Lord said to them next through his prophet Jeremiah? You got it. Verse 11—Plans to prosper. Plans for hope and a future.

Sometimes Disney World is not fifteen minutes away. Sometimes God lets us go to the bounce house. And when we find that out, we suddenly feel as though God isn't God—as though His love does not exist. But it not only exists, it is in motion.

As you approach the spider, whatever your spider is, approach it with this in mind: God has a plan, and God's plan to kill that bad boy is going to be much more precise than your plan. And, no, it isn't likely to take seventy years to kill your spider. But it is going to take you focusing on His face and listening to His every prompting as you wind your way down the corridor of cobwebs to your ultimate battle.

Listen to Him. Trust Him. Find power in Him. And slay that spider with Him.

What Are You Missing Simply Because You Aren't Walking with God on a Daily Basis?

We are human. That means we are going to get a lot of things wrong. We are going to think we have it all figured out and want to do things our way. Some of the time, we can get by on that. We might even manage to do some things really well. But the degree of blessing and the level of joy and awesomeness we can experience when God's plan is what we follow pales in comparison to anything we could concoct on our own. Don't cheat yourself out of God's richness by insisting you know a better way. Let Him give you Disney World and anything else that goes above and beyond your expectations.

- How have you been limiting God by insisting on following your own path?
- Can you imagine how much fuller your life could be if you let God lead you?
- What can you do today to start opening yourself up to where God wants you to go so you can track down your spider and kill it to make room for God's blessings?

BREAKTHROUGH

Not long after the Disney disaster, I was in therapy with Kenny, and it had been going great. Heather and I had worked our tails off to heal from the wounds inflicted a few years prior. We were growing in Jesus. We felt an insane amount of love for each other. Alas, even in this good season, I found myself at OnSite in an intensive therapy program.

It was now the next to last day. I had grown to actually love these people. Yes, these very same people who I was dreading spending six days locked in a tiny room baring my soul with, and I still didn't know their full names or what they did. This was absolutely mind-blowing to me, but it was so brilliant. This was also the day we found out what everybody actually did.

I thought the pharmacist was a construction worker.
I thought the multi-millionaire CEO was a ski
   instructor.
I thought the lady who owned a flower shop was a New
   York socialite.

I thought the stay-at-home dad was a writer. (Close enough)

I thought the full-time student was a professional athlete.

I thought the barista was a college professor.

Mind. Blown.

And you know what the greatest part of this eye-opening day was? Almost everybody in the group thought I was either a rapper or a poet! Incredible. This may be the last book I ever write because I'm gonna start droppin' some beats.

The days had been filled with tears and laughter, break-throughs and breakouts. Yes, somebody actually found a way to break their phone out of the prison that all the phones were kept in. That's how bad we are, people. We can't go without our phones for a few days. My phone was still locked up, so at this point I had not talked to anyone outside of our forty-person commune for six days. In all honesty, I didn't even want my phone back. I'd found a new safe place, where these were the people who knew me most. Every day, two people from our group of ten would do their "work." We had all role-played in each other's stories and were more than familiar with each other's wants and desires. Bill had told us at the beginning of the week, "These people will know you better than anyone on the planet," and by now I knew he was right. I had grown to love this group of ragamuffins—the very group of people I was so sure I couldn't stand only a week before.

This day was focused on "reentry." I don't remember if this was the official term, but it's what I would call it. We were concentrating on how to take these new life skills and use them away from OnSite. Basically, we were leaving the Narnia of emotional health. Everyone had experienced the breakthroughs and collected the tools they needed to better live their lives, myself included.

"Carlos," Nancy chimed in from the corner, "How have the last few days been for you?" I found this question kind of random. Nancy hadn't really been asking us questions like that this morning. It had been fairly informal. "I mean, fine, I guess," I replied. Why was she asking me this? Was I not fine? Was I acting weird?

"I know it's the next to last day, and I know that you have already done your group work, but I have a gut feeling that you need to have one more conversation."

I had the same feeling you get when you were called to the principal's office. I felt like I was in trouble. And who did she want me to have a conversation with? I had already gotten "real" with my mom, my dad, my brother, my wife, my kids, and my dog. Who was left?

"I think you need to have a conversation with God," Nancy continued.

God? What? Really? Nancy was not a Christian. In fact, she was *far* from it. She blatantly told us numerous times that she wasn't a Jesus person. She loved everybody, but that wasn't her thing. And the thing I loved about that is she hadn't given in to my Christian delicacy that week. None of my Christianese worked on her. I had to get past the lingo and to my core. And apparently she had gone with me because she was now asking me to role-play a conversation with God. This should be good.

"Team, Carlos needs to have a conversation with God,

so let's gather around and help him. Carlos, who would you like to play God?"

Man, I was not sure about this. Everything about this felt *really* sacrilegious. *I was going to have to pick somebody to play God? Was I about to get struck down by lightning? Was God about to turn all of us into pillars of salt?* But as I had with all the other exercises that week, I went along with it.

"Brian," I said. "Brian is to play God."

I had just found out only minutes earlier that Brian was the CEO of about four really huge companies I was familiar with. Brian also was ridiculously good-looking and had a beard. And since Jim Caviezel wasn't available, Brian would do.

Nancy took Brian to the opposite side of the room from where I was sitting, over by the door that led out of the room. Brian stood over there and Nancy told me to stay where I was. Then she walked over to her cabinet full of utensils— the same one where she found a bat for Sharon to use a few days prior when she swung at a rubber block while cussing me out. Well, not me, but her grandfather. I couldn't help but wonder what trick she had up her sleeve this time.

Nancy pulled out a towel. She also pulled out what looked like a black bandana. She walked over to Brian and pulled up a chair. She asked him to sit in the chair and whispered something in his ear. Then she did something creepy. The black bandana she pulled out of the magic drawer? It wasn't a bandana. It was a large silky handkerchief of some sort. It was slightly see through, but not completely. She draped that cloth over Brian's head. He was now sitting across from me, completely still, with black fabric over his entire head.

It was large enough that it draped all the way past his neck to his collarbone. I could barely make out his eyes beneath the black fabric. But that was it, just his eyes. If it had been nighttime, this would have been the stuff of nightmares.

But it wasn't a nightmare. And it wasn't scary. And it was the middle of the day. And Nancy was just beginning to paint on the canvas called my heart. "Carlos, come closer. I want you to do something for us. Look at God and just start talking to Him."

I could suddenly feel every eye in the room staring at me. I was so uncomfortable. I knew it was Brian. This wasn't gonna work.

"Um. Hey, God, it's me. What's up?" I immediately started chuckling along with a few others in the room. Even Nancy let out a chuckle, which surprised me because I knew this was supposed to be a serious exercise. But I just couldn't.

"That's okay, Carlos. Why don't you tell God why you are laughing? What's so funny?" Nancy calmly said.

"Well, God. I just . . . I mean, this is weird. It's kinda funny too. Brian looks like Jesus. That's why I picked him. Apparently, he is supposed to be You. I'm looking forward to what You have to say to me." Here's the thing. This entire time Brian was staring right at me, right into my eyes. I could kind of make out his mouth. He was smiling—not a laugh-at-me kind of smile, just a gentle smile. I started to feel more comfortable in the situation, so I kept going. "So, anyway, God. I've had a hell of a week. I mean, it's been good, but it's also been kinda crazy. You know what I'm talking about? The labyrinth. Yeah, what's up with that? Where did You go?"

By this point in my conversation, the eyes in the room began to disappear. Nancy kept walking back over to God and whispering things into His ears. I kept waiting for Him to reply. But He didn't. He just kept staring at me. Into me. I continued, "So, yeah, I'm a little bit confused right now, God. Because I kinda lost You back there. I mean, maybe it was before the labyrinth. Maybe it was awhile before then."

At this point, Nancy magically appeared next to me. She handed me a dish towel. "Keep talking. Keep it up. You are doing good, but I want you to start wringing this towel in your hands. I want you to start wringing it like it's wet, and you are trying to get all the water out while you are talking to God. Go ahead." So I did.

One wring. Two wrings. I could feel the hair begin to stand up on the back of my neck. And I could feel some sort of emotion beginning to rise inside of me. I didn't know quite yet if this was a good or a bad emotion, but I could tell it was a strong emotion.

"I just don't get it, God. I mean, You know I have been working for You for so long. For *so* long. And what do I get? I get to lose You? I get to lose you on top of a hill while a bagpipe is playing? I mean, if I'm being honest . . ." (At this point I could feel the volume in me rising. I wasn't shouting, but I was not talking quietly either.)

"Keep at it. Yes. Be honest. Be completely honest," Nancy interjected. I looked down at the towel in my hands. I don't even remember doing this, but the towel was in a knot. I had tied a knot so tight in it that I couldn't get it undone. "Keep talking, Carlos. Look back into God's eyes," Nancy encouraged.

"Yeah, if I'm being completely honest with You, God,

I don't know if I have felt You in a long time—way longer than a few days. Where have You been?" I continued in this frame of thought for about two minutes while Nancy secretly brought the magic bat and block to me. I'd been at OnSite long enough to know what to do with it. She simply handed it to me as I kept my prayer/conversation with God going. And going it was. Within two seconds, I was hitting that block with that bat as I was yelling.

"I don't feel You anymore. I haven't felt You in a long time! Huh? Where? I don't feel You when I sing these damn songs anymore. I don't feel You when I go to church any-more! Why? Why God? *Why did You disappear?* Where were You when I almost left my family? Where were You when my kids were weeping in the guest bedroom because they didn't know why Mommy had run out of the house crying and taken off in the car? Where were You when the Bergstrums came and took them from me saying, 'Heather knows. She wants the kids to come with us.' Where God? Where the hell are You?"

I was weeping. Uncontrollably. I was sobbing. I was yell-ing. I was cussing. I was so angry. I was so angry that God had left. In the middle of this rant, I was suddenly inter-rupted by a *"Stop!"* Nancy suddenly stopped my Niagara Falls of emotion from escaping my lungs and heart.

And God . . . He hadn't flinched. He hadn't moved. There He was. Sitting with a veil over His face, smiling softly at me.

"God, get up," Nancy ordered.

"Carlos, come here," Nancy called. I knew what she was gonna do. I'd seen her game. She was gonna get me and God to hug or something.

"Sit down. Right there, in the chair God was in."

So I sat down in God's chair. She grabbed God and walked Him over to where I was just standing, having a spiritual breakdown. She whispered in God's ear. Then she took the veil off His face. She carried the veil over to where I was sitting and delicately placed it over my head. I didn't know what was happening until two seconds later when "God" started talking, only God didn't have a veil on anymore, and God was staring at me saying this: "If I'm being honest with You, I don't know when the last time was that I felt You. It's been longer than a few days. Where have Ybeen, God?"

Wait a minute. Why was God asking me the same questions I had been asking Him only a few minutes earlier? What? Then God started yelling at me . . .

"I don't feel You anymore! I haven't felt You in years, God! Where? I don't feel You when I sing these church songs anymore, God. I don't feel You when I go to church! Why did You disappear, God?"

Halfway through Brian shouting at me, I realized what Nancy was doing. Brian wasn't God anymore. Brian was me.

"Where were You when I almost left my family, God? Where were You when my kids were crying and scared to death because Mommy ran off crying, God? Where were You when they took my kids from me, God?! Where the hell are You, God?"

Nancy yelled for him to stop. Then she looked at me. I could still see Nancy through my veil. She had such a peaceful presence. And then she spoke, "Can You answer him, God?"

And without any more prompting, I felt such a peace

wash over me. Such a peace. And breath began to escape my lungs carrying these words: "I was with you when she left, Carlos. I was with you when you felt so alone. I have been with you. Did you not see Me in the way Sohaila danced on her days with you? I was there in her dance. I was in Losiah's giggle and laughter. I was with Seanna as she cried for you, and I gave her comfort. I was there in the sunset when you walked out of the church service where you did not feel Me. I was right there. I was right there in the Scriptures in your backpack you never took out when the preacher would give his message. I've been right here all along, Carlos. I was here. I am here. I never left."

All of that came out of me so smoothly, so fluently. And I was staring right into Brian's eyes the entire time.

When I was finished, Nancy stood me up and walked me over to where Brian was. She took the veil off of my face. She walked Brian back over to the chair I had just been sitting in. She put the veil back on Brian's head. She didn't even need to whisper to Brian what he needed to do. Like clockwork, Brian began speaking back to me what God had already spoken to me, through me.

"Carlos, I was with you . . ."

Tears began to flood my eyes as I heard God reminding me that He was always there. He had never gone. He had never left. I was just looking in the wrong places. I was looking where I had always been told to look, but I had not been gazing up. I had been gazing at life and only glancing up at God.

And the anger and frustration inside of my soul, it left. I fell to the ground, crying tears of joy. I had found God. I had a time line in my shouting match with God that told me exactly where I made agreements with Satan that I was abandoned. And I told myself that, if I was abandoned by God, then what did life matter anyway? What difference would it make if I found my identity in anything and everything else?

As I was on the floor crying, I could feel the hands of my small group begin to touch me. They began to rub my back. They began to reach under my arms and lift me up. When I stood up, I opened my eyes. Nancy's eyes were about two inches from mine.

"I think you just found your spider. You believed the lie that God had abandoned you. Truth is, He's been here all along."

What If He Has Been with You All Along?

It isn't uncommon to feel disconnected from God when things are not going smoothly in life. It's even likely that you may feel abandoned entirely when things start going wrong. It is normal for those feelings to come up, because you are vulnerable and that's when the enemy loves to strike. He wants to get you to believe he has won. The important thing is not to come into agreement with him on this lie. It can be tough when you are in the midst of a crisis to see past the pain and fear, but that is exactly how you avoid falling under the influence of the enemy. Gaze upward at God, and the things of life that are clouding your judgment will dissipate.

- What lies do you believe about God's presence in your life?

- Are there things you can see in your life, no matter how small, that can serve as a kind of GPS to help you locate God?
- Looking back at crisis moments ... ask God, "Where were You in that moment?" Now, listen and trust.

KILL THE SPIDER

What. A. Moment.

God was there. All along. After Nancy spoke that truth to me, I left that room in a sort of trance. I was so relieved. So grateful. I had spent the last few days wandering in this maze of uncertainty, with the only light being Bill's constant reminder to "Trust the process. Celebrate the miracle." That process had led me straight to it. Straight to my spider.

Now, let me shoot straight with you.

I do not just have one spider.

My OnSite experience was super intense. It took six days of therapy to get to this one spider. As complex as our human souls are, each of us likely has more than one spider. More than one lie will stand between us and who we were intended to be.

Not every spider is a big, hairy, bubbly-eyed, bench-pressing, arachnophobia-inducing monster waiting in the darkest corner of my soul.

I have believed more than one lie in my lifetime, and not

all of them were huge and massively destructive. Sometimes there are little ones. Those pesky mini lies might be as damaging on a daily basis as the he-man-looking ones you have to dig out during therapy. A lie is a lie. And our God is a God of truth.

More on this in a moment.

So it was Thursday. Thursday at lunch. I was floating. I had done it. Thanks to my time with these amazing people on this beautiful farm, I had found the reasons I'd been medicating. Discovered cobwebs I didn't know existed. I had traced those cobwebs to a spider, and I had looked the spider in the eyes and realized the massive lie that had messed up my life. This last day sort of reminds me of the last scene in a really good Disney movie. Everything and everyone is a little more colorful than they had been. I was all but certain I could faintly hear the *Lion King* sound track coming from the Tennessee hills behind the farm. The day was filled with "Hakuna Matata."

When I got back to my room after lunch, I pulled out my OnSite binder filled with all my notes and learnings from the week and began thumbing through it. So. Much. Goodness. It was like a manual on life. I know, I know. The binder was not the Bible. But it was definitely second for me in terms of transformation. I knew that I would be coming back to this notebook for years to come. I was thumbing through the pages when I got to the schedule for the week. It had been a few days since I had seen it because, well, the days became routine. But I noticed something I hadn't noticed before. I thought the program was over the next morning, but it was finishing that night!

I had a mild panic attack. A good one. It was filled with,

OMG. OMG. Heather can come pick me up tonight? There's no way I'm staying here tonight if I can go home! But where is she? Is she even in town? What if she can't come and get me?

You should know something about my family. We don't stay put. We stick the kids in the minivan at a moment's notice and drive two days to Colorado just to watch the sunset over the Rockies. It would not have been out of the question for my wife to have been gone. Literally. With no cell signal at the top of some mountain. I'd had zero contact with her for six days.

I ran out of my cabin to look for Bill. I found him soothing some beautiful soul next to the horseshoe pit. "Bill! So sorry to interrupt. When can we get our phones back? Now?" I jumped into his convo with zero shame in my game.

"Soon," he replied. "What's up?"

I filled him in on my recent discovery that this Narnia was ending twelve hours earlier than I thought. It didn't matter because most people here lived all over the planet. But I happened to be one of the only locals, and I was about to hitchhike home if I had to.

"I see. We are giving you back your phones next session. You can call your wife then."

Within the hour, I was holding my five and a half inches of LCD in my left hand.

I wasn't expecting the anxiety that rushed over me.

I had just spent a week with no access to anyone else but those on this journey with me. I had just spent a week completely disconnected from any sort of envy, doubt, or desires that social media had been imposing on my soul. I didn't realize how heavy that phone would feel. I had to turn it on in order to call Heather. "Just turn it on, Carlos. You got this," I whispered to myself.

I turned on my iPhone and watched the top left corner of my screen blink and spatter as it searched for a signal. Bing. Bing. BING. BINGBINGBINGBING. The notifications came rushing in. But I didn't open one message. I simply went to the phone app and dialed Heather.

When it began to ring, I had about 231 thoughts fly through my head. What if she decided she was done with me this week, and I didn't know it? What if she is in Montana or somewhere? What if . . .

"Hello? Daddy?" It was Seanna, my beautiful middle child. And without warning, I simply began to weep uncontrollably. "Daddy? Are you there? Is it you?" she asked.

"Yes, baby. It's me. It's me. Where are you? Where are you guys? Are you home? Where's Mom? Is she with you? Can I talk to her?" I rambled through tears, snot, and joy.

"She's right here! We're home," Seanna said.

And with those three words, I could breathe again. They were home. Eighty minutes from where I was standing.

"Hey! How are you calling me? How did you get your phone?" It was Heather now. OMG, I missed her.

"I messed up the schedule. It's over tonight. Can you come? Can you come tonight and get me?" Heather heard the desperation in my voice.

"Of course. I have Natalie's littles. Can they come? Nat and JT are on a date and I'm babysitting."

"Of course. Bring them. Bring the neighborhood. Bring the dog and cat. I don't care. *Just get here.*"

I was overwhelmed with the thought of seeing my family. I couldn't believe this was happening. I was going home.

I couldn't believe that I found my spider.

I couldn't believe that I had made it through the week.

I couldn't believe I was better.

I couldn't believe my luck.

"Can you be here at eight? That's about when we will be done with our final session."

"Of course. See you soon," she replied.

I dropped my phone on my bed and began to weep. Again. Hi, I'm Carlos. And I now officially cry. A lot.

The final session was such a celebration. All forty of us were in a room celebrating the healing that had happened. We went around in a circle and shared. People who were suicidal on Saturday were now full of hope and life. People who were chronic liars were filled with more truth than they knew what to do with. When the circle moment came to me, I said it. I said it with a twist of French normally reserved for sailors. "I did it, guys. I killed my spider. I killed my @#$%&! spider!" and cheers swept the room. My soul was picked up and passed around like the winning coach at the end of the championship game. After the cheering, and as I listened to a few others in the circle share their healings, something hit me hard. Not in a bad way. Not in a sad way. But in a truth bomb kinda way.

I had found my spider. Yes.

But had I killed it?

I didn't think I had. Not yet.

I had searched for it. I had found it. I had cornered it.

But it was going to take something more than what OnSite could give me to kill it. And I knew exactly what it was. Exactly *who* it was.

His name was Jesus. And He had the sword I needed to chop this thing in half.

After our final session, Heather and the kids pulled up.

In a mix of tears and snot, I introduced them to my entire small group. My group was huggin' them like they had known them for years. And they actually kinda had. In a matter of one week, these nine human beings knew more about me than almost any human on the planet. My family was overjoyed and overwhelmed all at once. In the midst of my jubilee, I caught a glimpse from Heather, a look of "Who are these people and why are they hugging my children?"

I hugged my OnSite family good-bye and got in the driver's side seat in our Honda Odyssey. It was quiet in the car. Almost like nobody knew what to say or how to act.

"It was good," I said. "It was good," I said again. All the while thinking, "I've found it. Now let's get home and kill it."

I turned onto Highway 40 headed east. Heather reached over and grabbed my hand. She didn't say anything. She didn't have to. The way she squeezed my hand told me all I needed to know. She was all in. Little did I know how much I would need her for this final battle with my spider. Little did I know.

When You Don't Know How to Move Forward

I know I've said it a few times already, but you don't have to go to seven days of therapy to pull off this sort of discovery.

Here is a simple yet effective prayer I pray when I need God to reveal something inside of me that I simply cannot find without Him.

Jesus, I come to You now to be made whole
with You again. I come to You now, asking

to be restored and renewed in You this day.
I come to You to claim the grace and mercy
You have waiting for me. I now surrender
every aspect of who I am, who I have been,
and who I will be totally to You, Lord.

After centering myself with God and asking Him to make me who I need to be in Him again, I move on to the next part:

Thank You, Jesus, for being here. I invite
You to come in and show me that place
where my heart was shattered. Come in and
show me that place where I was wounded.
Come in and show me that place where I
made an agreement with a lie that has kept
me bound. Jesus, maybe shoot me a memo-
ry or a word. Come for me, Jesus, and show
me that place.

Now that you have prayed that, listen. Sit and listen, and see where the Lord takes your thoughts. It helps in these kinds of prayer sessions to have a journal. Write down where He is taking you. It may seem way off, which is fine. Write it down. Don't edit what comes to mind. Just write it down. Write down any wounds (especially from your childhood) that come to mind. Ask God to reveal to you the lie you made an agreement with at that point. Remember, there may be more than one lie.

This isn't a one-and-done kind of situation. We have to continue to go at it. Just because you don't get a thought at first, don't give up! It's there. There are many other ways to get to the root, but the first step is opening ourselves up to prayer. And if you haven't been used to praying, don't feel like you have to get it the first time. You wouldn't show up at a gym for the first time or after a long break and expect to be able to run a marathon or bench 250 lbs. Keep at it, friends. We are getting close.

WEAPONS OF WAR

I tried to hold back. I really did. One of Bill's last recommendations to all of us on the final night was simple. "You guys have grown so much. You have learned so much. I can see it in your eyes. You are leaning against that starting gate and are ready to let all of this new knowledge spill all over your world. You are ready to live a centered life and help everyone around you live theirs as well. But be careful. You don't know it yet, but you have what I like to call OnSite goggles over your eyes. You will leave this place and suddenly see everyone's medicators. Remember, this is about *you* getting back to the center of *your* life. Not theirs."

Oh, how true this was. In the following few days, it was incredible what I was seeing in people's lives. In my friends' lives. In my family's lives. And it was so hard to not stop them and help them out of that unhealthy spot. And so I bit my tongue and kept looking inward. Well, with everyone except Heather. The poor woman got three days' worth of nonstop unpacking.

But she signed up for this.

Kinda.

"So now what?" Heather asked as we drove down I-40.

I was a bit put off by her question. Now what? Now what? I'll tell you now what. Now I'm a centered man. You are living with an incredible human being. That's now what.

That's what I thought quietly. But that's not what I said.

"Um. I dunno. What do you think?"

That's what I said. Eloquently. Just like that.

"How do we keep this going? You are close. Don't give up now."

She was right. I wasn't done. I was close, but I wasn't done.

I knew what she and I both needed. We needed to see the spider dead. We hadn't started talking about it that way, with that language yet, but we knew what was needed. I told her for sure I wouldn't give up.

There was a freshness to my faith the following few months. Everything felt brand-new. After losing my faith on a Tuesday and finding it again on a Friday, it looked completely different. Scripture was new. Old passages popped. I was entering this new season in my faith where I was literally "hearing" God in new ways. He was *talking*. To me. I know, I know. We say that stuff all the time. I had said that stuff in the past. But something was different now. Something had changed. I was *hearing* God so clearly. I was hearing Him not only when I would read Scripture but when I was doing the most random things.

I was realizing that when my soul was refreshed, when my spirit was rested, I was hearing from God more clearly. And I'm not talking about living in a constant state of vacation. I was hustling hard. But in the hustle, I was making sure that I was rested and refreshed so that I could keep hearing from God the way I was intended to.

Case in point . . .

A few months after OnSite, my wife and I were on our way back from our fifteen-year wedding anniversary trip to Ireland. It was filled with lots of refreshment, but not a lot of rest. We had moments, waking up in a tiny cottage on some farm in Ireland overlooking sheep and goats grazing. There was rest in those moments, but then we would rush out to explore. The refreshing came, but you know how at the end of a good vacation, sometimes you need a vacation from the vacation? That was where we found ourselves.

We had landed in Detroit for a final layover before heading home to Nashville and had stopped at P.F. Chang's for dinner. We had been traveling for over fifteen hours already and were basically the walking dead—zombies with little, if anything, motivating us to speak. But, for some reason, I decided to tell her a story about a guy I had met the week prior in London. He was a former atheist who told this hilarious story about playing percussion for a worship leader friend of his while shaking a banana shaker. I'll spare you the details of the story because, come to think of it, it wasn't really funny at all; Heather didn't even smile. In one ear and out the other.

"Babe? You get it? A banana shaker?"

Fine. Forget it. I'm done trying to make small talk. It's obvious we just need to get home.

I don't know if I have ever on purpose told a story where the central theme was a banana. Maybe a knock-knock joke in third grade where the punch line was "Orange you glad I didn't say banana?" But that's it. And that was thirty years ago.

I finished the banana story and Heather did not laugh. Then she cracked open her fortune cookie. Her eyes got huge.

"What is it? Good fortune?" I asked.

She flipped the fortune over so I could read it. There was only one word written on it: Banana.

We both started laughing that sort of incredibly annoying public laughter.

How many fortune cookies carry a fortune that simply say banana? *It said banana.*

I started having a worship moment right then and there. I almost stood to my feet and led the entire restaurant in "Oceans." *God is here*, I thought. *He just gave me a fortune with the word banana!*

"He's reminding us that He is in the ordinary. He is paying attention. He's playful," Heather said. I mean there it is. Do you believe it? I do! God is in the ordinary, everyday moments of life. We just have to be rested or refreshed enough to be able to hear Him!

Then I cracked my cookie open. The author of the smashing breakthrough book *Moment Maker* opened his cookie. (It had been a year since its release.) It had one word on it: Moment.

Are you serious?

Coincidence over. God obviously was laughing with me. He is in the ordinary. I mean, God was hanging out in my fortune cookie, just smiling at me as I sat in amazement.

So if God is in the ordinary—the everyday—then why have I not been taught this? If God still speaks so clearly, why have I missed it? I used to think this stuff was crazy. Bananas, if you will.

God is for sure in the majestic, yes. God sometimes shows up in a blaze of glory. But God is also surrounding us in conversation every single day. We just don't recognize Him. We believe in a God who can heal our cancer and raise the dead, but we don't believe we can ask Him for something trivial? This places us in a conundrum. We have to stop thinking God is only in the sky and the heavens. He's in our cars, in our homes, and in our cafes. We have to pay attention. We get to rest in that truth and keep our eyes open and our hearts attentive.

Over and over again, God keeps showing up like that. Over and over again, He kept showing up to me when I would seek Him. I'd ask Him a question, and He would lead me to a Scripture that answered me specifically. All of a sudden, my relationship with God was getting way more detailed than I ever thought it could be.

Not long after the banana incident, I found myself in London, England. I was there for a conference but had landed a day early so that I could write.

I had managed to have a fairly drama-free existence since OnSite. I was growing in my relationship with God, I was growing in my roles as husband, father, and friend, but I still had not come face to face with this spider. I was almost running from the battle. I knew where to look, but I didn't wanna.

One can only run so long.

My lie. God had abandoned me. That lie had sent me to some of the darkest places I had ever been. That lie had destroyed my marriage. That lie had caused more anxiety in my life than anyone should have to deal with. But in the newness of my fresh faith, I had uncovered some solid truths about God's power over darkness and how He does and will come to our rescue when we need it. We simply have to ask Him. He has given us authority.

When I landed in London, I got a call from Heather. Something was wrong with one of the kids, and she didn't know what to do. The second I heard concern in her voice, I could feel the blood rushing from my limbs to my heart. I could feel my heart rapidly rise up in my throat. "I'm coming home, Babe. I can't be here and helpless. I'm coming home on the next flight," I said in a panic.

"No. Don't. Talk to Jesus. Ask Him what to do," she said with a peace that my heart needed at the moment.

"Okay. Okay." I hung up. I may have said I would talk to Jesus, but my mind went everywhere else. I was a nine-hour flight from my family when they needed me. What did I do? I started Googling symptoms to the health condition my kid was in. I started down that dark, dark hole. My mind was racing. I needed something to calm my heart, and I tried to create that peace myself. I needed to find some article somewhere telling me that everything was going to be okay.

The entire train ride from Heathrow to my hotel, I Googled. With every click, the pace of my heart grew faster. The darkness in my soul grew darker. I knew I needed Jesus, but I felt paralyzed by fear. I didn't know what to do.

I arrived at my hotel room completely and totally overwhelmed by panic and fear. I had not felt this in years.

As I lay in my bed overlooking some picturesque street in the heart of London, I just started crying. And in those tears came a sort of heart cry prayer that we find in the Psalms of David.

"Dear Jesus. I'm done being scared, Jesus. Please Jesus.

I feel so alone. Where are You Lord?! Why is this happening to my family, Jesus? Dear Lord, please. Please help."

That was the sort of snot-filled prayer that was escaping my lungs. The sort of prayer that isn't filled with faith as much as it's filled with doubt. And in my case, doubt that God had abandoned my family. Again.

Right there. It hit me. My mind went rushing back to OnSite. My mind went rushing back to how and when I found God again. Maybe, just maybe He was right there then too. Maybe I was not alone. Dear Lord, I thought I was done with this!

I cried myself to sleep. When I woke up, it was dark outside. I had slept my afternoon away. I was supposed to be writing my book. I was supposed to be writing my book helping people kill their spiders and there I was, lying in the middle of a cobweb so thick I didn't know how to get out of it.

"Just get up," I thought to myself. "Get up and go have dinner."

I got up and reluctantly left my tiny hotel room. While I still had Wi-Fi, I FaceTimed Heather. It was morning in Nashville. She answered. I was hoping she would answer saying that everything was better and we were worried about nothing. That's not what she said.

"It's getting a bit worse. I'm gonna call the doctor and see if we can't get squeezed in earlier." I thought my anxiety couldn't reach new levels. It did. *Dear God, if you can put the word* banana *into a fortune cookie, could you please just show up here?* My anxiety was turning into anger.

"Have you asked God yet, Carlos? Have you talked with Him?" she asked.

You know what's crazy? I hadn't. *Still*. How are humans so stubborn?

"No, Babe. I haven't asked Him if I should come home. I haven't asked how to fix this with our kid," I answered.

"That's not what you should be asking. Have you asked Him to kill this lie inside of you that He is not here? He is here, Carlos. Me and the kids feel Him all around this situation. We are fine. You, on the other hand. You are tangled. I'm going to pray for you. I think it's time. I think it's time you killed it."

Wow.

I said good-bye and grabbed this little book on spiritual warfare that I had been studying the last few months. There was a section in the back of the book that dealt specifically with the power of prayer in healing that I had skimmed over a few times yet never really sat in. I walked out the door of the hotel. It was cold, so I put on my gloves and turned left. There was a little square not far from the hotel that had some stores, cafes, and restaurants. I found a little Indian restaurant that had only five tables and, by the looks of it, they had just opened. I walked in and sat at a table. Sipping on my tea and water, I started reading the book.

A final word: Be strong in the Lord and in his mighty power. Put on all of God's armor so that you will be able to stand firm against all strategies of the devil. For we are not fighting against flesh-and-blood enemies, but against evil rulers and authorities of the unseen world, against mighty powers in this dark world, and against evil spirits in the heavenly places.

Therefore, put on every piece of God's armor so

you will be able to resist the enemy in the time of evil. Then after the battle you will still be standing firm. Stand your ground, putting on the belt of truth and the body armor of God's righteousness. For shoes, put on the peace that comes from the Good News so that you will be fully prepared.

In addition to all of these, hold up the shield of faith to stop the fiery arrows of the devil. Put on salvation as your helmet, and take the sword of the Spirit, which is the word of God.

Pray in the Spirit at all times and on every occasion. Stay alert and be persistent in your prayers for all believers everywhere.

EPHESIANS 6:10–18 NLT

"Then after the battle you will be standing firm."

Man, I needed this like yesterday. I felt anything but firm.

The waiter came, and I asked him for the most flavorful curry dish they had. And make it spicy. He obliged, and I went back into the book.

The author of this book was talking about the power that the name of Jesus has. In so many prayers we tack on, right before Amen, "In the name of Jesus." It's almost become an afterthought. But the author was reminding us of the true power—that the God who makes the earth spin and float, that God, gives us His authority and power. It's just up to us to use it. The author called up this passage.

At that time you won't need to ask me for anything. I tell you the truth, you will ask the Father directly, and he will grant your request because you use my name.

You haven't done this before. Ask, using my name,
and you will receive, and you will have abundant joy.

JOHN 16:23-24 NLT

Right here? In this restaurant? Is this where I'm going to go after it? I couldn't think of a better place. I was so exhausted from the worry and fear that had been crippling me for years. I was so tired from the twelve-hour battle with anxiety and fear I'd had since I landed. I had no shame doing battle with this lie that God had abandoned me while wiping curry from my lips.

I put the book down when my food arrived. It tasted *so* good. I was all in. This prayer I was about to pray was gonna have to wait, cause this curry was all up in my grill.

"Is there any way I could get some hot sauce? It's not spicy enough," I told the waiter. He came back a few seconds later with a smirk on his face.

I dripped a few drops on my rice and stirred it around. By this point there were a few other patrons in the restaurant. I took two bites of my freshly hot sauce—anointed rice when the sweat began to drip off my dome. *Wow.* The man did me right. This was *hot.*

I grabbed my water to quench the fire in my throat, but as I swallowed I noticed that the water wasn't going down as easily as it should. Weird.

I took another bite of rice and felt it get stuck on the way down my pipe. I grabbed my water and tried to wash it down. The water not only got stuck behind the rice, it immediately came back up into my mouth and I covered my mouth and ran to the bathroom. I still did it in a pretty discreet manner as to not alarm anyone that I was *dying.*

I spit out the water and the rice that had slowly worked its way back up my throat. What was happening? I could feel my throat now. You aren't supposed to be able to feel your throat. It could feel it swelling up. I could feel it tickling. I looked in the mirror and in a panic realized that I was having some sort of allergic reaction to the hot sauce. Somehow, as I was fumbling up the stairs to the bathroom I had butt dialed Heather. She heard it all, but I had no idea she was on the phone. I can only imagine her hearing me gag and freak out on the other end of the phone. After I collected myself, I pulled out my wallet, dropped some cash on the table, grabbed my book, and sped out of the restaurant. I needed to find a drug store and some Benadryl stat.

I was panicked. Again. Feeling alone and lost in a big city on the other side of the planet from home. My God. This is crazy. The second I was about to go after this spider, I have an allergic reaction to hot sauce?

I pulled out my phone to call my wife to ask her what to do. My God, I felt so alone.

I was sprinting down the sidewalk when she finally answered.

"Is everything okay? I heard you choking or something on the phone," she surprisingly said.

"Really? I'm having an allergic reaction and need to find a drug store. I'll call you back, okay?" I said.

"Okay," she said with worry in her voice.

My panic was growing as I could feel my throat closing even more. About five minutes down the street, I found a drug store and some Benadryl. I pulled it off the shelf and ripped it open and swallowed it right there. I walked to the counter with a ripped open package and the store clerk cautiously rang me up. I'm sure I looked like a madman. He gave me my change and I started walking back to my hotel. Alone.

How was this even real? Was my spider actually trying to kill *me* before I killed it? When I got to my room, I was blubbering again. I was undone. The stress of the day and then the stress of the evening came pouring out of me. This was so obviously a spiritual attack taking shape in physical form. It was no longer theory. It was no longer just an idea.

I needed Jesus to come into that tiny hotel room right then. I was desperate.

I picked up my Bible and the book I had been reading and started praying out loud exactly as it was laid out.

"True and living God, Jesus, I come to You to be made new in You again. I come to You to be brought back to the truth of who You are. That lie that You had left? I know for sure it is a complete and total lie from the enemy and I reject it. Forgive me. By the cross of Jesus Christ, I bring the full work of the cross against this lie. Jesus, I want Your voice to be the only voice to speak into this space. Lord, freedom and the breaking of my agreement with this lie will only come from You. Jesus, cut off, bind, and send the spider and all webs created by this spider to the foot of the cross for You to deal with as You wish. I send it to You, Jesus. Do with it as You please. Come now, Jesus, come rushing into the chasm in my heart that this lie was trying to fill. Let the truth of You and the light of You come and fill the space that feeling of abandonment left vacant. Dear Jesus, show me truth. Replace the hole in my spirit with the truth of my marriage, my wife, my children, my ministry, my life. Jesus, fill this broken and empty space in my heart. In the name of Jesus Christ, I pray. Amen."

And then I started sending anything that was attacking me mentally, physically, and spiritually to the foot of the cross. I was using the power and authority of Jesus to send that crap away. I was fighting. I was swinging.

By this point, I found myself in the shower. Weeping and praying.

Confessing. Renouncing. Rejecting. Replacing.

Confessing. Renouncing. Rejecting. Replacing.

Confessing. Renouncing. Rejecting. Replacing.

That was it. It was done. There was no more power in the lie. My spider had me no more. The spider was dead.

Was it magic? No. Was it a one-time prayer? No. Did striving produce results? No. Did Jesus absolutely take my prayer and begin to deal with this spider, crushing it and sending it into the abyss of His judgment? Absolutely.

Here is what happened in that prayer.

1. Confess

We need to agree with God that we have not only been believing the lie, but we have lost our belief in God's truth. This is of utmost importance. We must come clean and ask forgiveness for our unbelief in God's promises about who we are, who God is, His plans for our lives, and His truth about our futures. Start there.

2. Renounce

Now that we have asked for forgiveness for our unbelief in God and our belief in this lie, we get to look this lie (the spider) in the eye and renounce it. By renouncing or rejecting it, we are refusing to abide by it any longer.

Jesus can hear us no matter how we pray. But to leave no stone unturned, I love to pray this out loud, telling the enemy. Even if you whisper it, pray this with the authority that has been given to you by Jesus. Pray it with confidence. Renounce the lie that has been keeping you bound in chains for so long.

3. Reject

This is the point in the prayer where the spider will literally flee. The dagger will sink deep within its heart and you will, with this language, step into a truth that you have not known for a long time.

It's very important that you be as specific here as you can. Reject every lie that Jesus has revealed to you.

4. Replace

Whenever you take something away, you must replace it with something else or you will have a void—a gap. That is why we must quickly refill the space in our spirit that this lie has vacated. The enemy will try to fill it with something if we don't. Ask Jesus to come heal and restore this place.

Be open. With this type of work, God will be speaking to you. Take a deep breath, remind yourself that you serve a God of the impossible, and write down what you feel the Lord is telling you.

When I was swinging at my massive spider, I had to go back to the moment that I let terror into my heart. I prayed to break the agreement that I made with terror and fear, and I renounced, rejected, and sent it to the foot of the cross. And I kept at it. I kept swinging at it, and guess what? I killed it.

IT'S YOUR TURN

Knowledge of the difference between cobwebs and spiders is a *very powerful* thing. But we have to be careful we don't start our own Spiritual Pest Control Service. That would be tempting—to use all this knowledge to go and rid the world of spiders! And as heroic as that thought may be, we must remember that we have to start with ourselves.

This power we have been given—the power from Jesus Christ Himself—is going to be necessary on a daily basis for us. The knowledge we have is going to come in handy almost every single day. For me it *is* every single day.

The attacks have not stopped as I have tried to finish this book. But instead of simply stressing when they come, I stress with a smile. Because I now know, and you now know the plan the enemy has. We can read it for ourselves in Scripture. With this knowledge comes freedom. Freedom to win. Freedom to thrive.

Just this morning I was on the phone with my dad, telling him that I am on the very last chapter of the book. And just as he piped in at the beginning of this book with, "Carlos, you need to kill the spider in your life," he piped in with another story. And I haven't missed the beautiful symmetry of my ending this book with another analogy from my dad.

As I shared the line about "stressing with a smile" with him, he shared this gem.

"Have you watched the movie *Patton*?" he asked me.

Of course I have not. Who watches movies from the '60s about a war from the '40s?

He continued, "Did you know that in the middle of a battle between Patton's army and Field Marshal Rommel in World War II, it's reported that General Patton, in a counterattack, yelled out, 'I read your book, Rommel! I read your book!' as the US Army destroyed the German army. Patton somehow got access to the enemy's plan of attack. He was going into that battle knowing exactly what Field Marshal Rommel's plans were. So he went into the attack with total confidence. And he won! This is why you can 'stress with a smile.'"

My dad was telling me that no matter our situation, we know the outcome.

> In order that Satan might not outwit us. For we are not unaware of his schemes.
>
> 2 CORINTHIANS 2:11

We know. We've read the enemy's book. We know he is going to attack us, and we know where in our lives we are the most susceptible. So you can go into the battle against every single spider in your life knowing that you will win.

We live in a world at war. The war won't end until Christ comes for His bride. But the battles in the war? The epic battles with these spiders that will continue to try to take us down? Those battles within the war, we can win. You will win. And on the other side of those victories is freedom like nothing you have ever tasted or seen.

It's your turn. Pull the sword out. It's time to swing.

A FINAL PRAYER

One of the tools that keeps my spiders at bay is a prayer that my wife and I pray every single day. I pray it first thing in the morning. We initially got this prayer from John Eldredge and have slowly adapted it to our lives over the years. Praying it daily is a great way to be intentional about remaining in daily intimacy with Jesus. It speaks to what is *true* of us in Christ. It has been the most powerful practical thing that has kept my spiders at bay. I have found that covering my life with the blood of the cross, the power of the resurrection, and the authority of His ascension is extremely valuable in my daily battle with the enemy, and I hope that this prayer helps you as well.

Take it. Pray it. Believe it.

Father, Christ, & Spirit . . .

I come to be restored in You, renewed in You, and brought back to receive Your love and Your life and all the grace and mercy I need this day. I honor You as my King and give every aspect of my life totally and completely to You. I give You my spirit, soul, body, mind, heart, and will. In all that I pray I include [name your immediate family members] acting as the head of my family I bring them under Your authority and covering. I cover them with Your blood—cover their spirits, souls, bodies, minds, hearts, and wills. I ask Your spirit to restore them in You, renew them in You, apply to them all that I now pray on their behalf.

Dear God Holy and victorious Trinity, You alone are worthy of all my worship, my heart's devotion, my praise, all my trust, and all the glory of my life. I love You, I worship You. I trust You. You alone are life, and You have become my life. I renounce all other Gods and idols [list those things that you have put your trust in], and I give You the place in my heart and my life that You truly deserve.

I confess here and now, God, that this is all about You and not about me. You are the hero of this story, and I belong to You. Forgive me for my every sin. Search me and know me and reveal to me where You are working in my life. In the name of Jesus Christ, I ask You to reveal to me any lies or vows and strongholds that contradict Your word and will. Grant me the grace of Your healing and deliverance and Your deep and true repentance. Thank You for loving me and choosing me before You made the world. I give myself over to You to be one with You in everything, as Jesus is one with You. Thank You for proving Your love by sending Jesus. I receive Him and all His life. Thank You for including me in Christ, for forgiving me my sins, for granting me His righteousness, and for making me complete in Him. Thank You for making me alive with Christ!

I bring the life and work of the Lord Jesus Christ over my life today; over my home, my family, my household; over all my kingdom and domain.

Jesus, thank You for coming, for being human like me. I love You. I trust You. I worship You. I give myself over to You to be one with You in all things—spirit, soul, body, mind, heart, and will. I receive all the work and triumph of Your cross, death, blood, and sacrifice, through which my every sin is atoned for. I am ransomed and delivered from the kingdom of darkness and transferred to Your kingdom. My sin nature is removed, my heart has been changed by the Holy Spirit, and every claim being made against me is canceled and disarmed this day. I now take my place in Your cross and death, dying with You to sin, to my flesh, to this world. I take up the cross and crucify my pride, arrogance, unbelief, lack of trust and faith [and anything else you are currently struggling with].

I put off the old [insert your name here]. Apply to me and my family all the work and triumph of Your blood and sacrifice. I receive it all with thanks and give it total claim to my spirit, soul, body, mind, heart, and will.

I bring the blood and sacrifices of Jesus Christ over my life today, over my home, my family, my household, my vehicles, finances, over all my kingdom and domain. I bring the cross, death, blood, and sacrifices of Jesus Christ against Satan, against his kingdom, against every foul and unclean spirit, every foul power. I bring the cross, death, blood and sacrifice of Jesus Christ to the borders of my kingdom and domain, and I stake it there in the name of Jesus Christ.

Jesus, I also receive You as my life. I receive all the work and power of Your resurrection through which You have conquered sin, death, judgment, and the enemy. Death has no power over You, nor does any foul thing. I have been raised with You to new life, dead to sin and alive to God. With my family, I take my place now in Your resurrection and in Your life. I receive Your hope, love, joy, goodness, wisdom, power, and strength. Apply to me and my family all the work and triumph in Your resurrection.

I bring the resurrection of the Lord Jesus Christ over my life today; over my home, my family, my household, finances, vehicles; over all my kingdom and domain. I bring the resurrection and the empty tomb of Jesus Christ against Satan, against his kingdom, against every foul and unclean spirit, against every human being and their spirit, their warfare and their household.

I bring the resurrection and the empty tomb of the Lord Jesus Christ to the borders of my kingdom and domain and I stake it there in the name of Jesus Christ.

Jesus I also receive You as my authority, rule, and dominion. My everlasting victory against Satan and his kingdom and my ability to bring Your kingdom at all times in every way. I receive all the work and triumph of Your ascension through which Satan has been judged and cast down, and all authority in heaven and on earth has been given to You. I take my place now in Your authority and in Your throne which I have been raised by You to the right hand of the Father and established in Your authority. I give myself to You. Apply to me and my family all the work and triumph in Your authority and in Your throne. I give it total claim to my spirit, soul, body, mind, heart, and will.

I now bring the authority of Jesus Christ over my life today; over my home, family, household, vehicles, and finances; over all my kingdom and domain. I now bring the authority, rule, and dominion of the Lord Jesus Christ against Satan, against his kingdom, against every foul and unclean spirit— every ruler, power, authority, and spiritual force of wickedness, their every weapon claim and device. [Name any foul spirits attacking you.] I send all foul and unclean spirits to the foot of the cross for Jesus to deal with, together with every backup and replacement, every weapon, claim, and device, by the authority of the Lord Jesus Christ and in His name. I command the judgment of the Lord Jesus Christ on any spirit that refuses to obey and send them to judgment by the authority of the Lord Jesus Christ and in His name.

Holy Spirit, thank You for coming. I love You, I worship You. I trust You. You have clothed me with power on high and sealed me in Christ. You have become my union with the Father, my counselor, comforter, strength and guide. I honor You as Lord and fully give You every aspect of my life totally and completely to You. Fill me, fresh Holy Spirit. Restore my union with the Father and Son. I receive You with thanks and give You total claim to my life.

Heavenly Father, thank You for granting to us every spiritual blessing in Christ Jesus. I claim the riches in Christ over my life today and over my family. I bring the blood of Christ once more over each of us—our spirits, souls, bodies, minds, hearts, and wills.

I put on the full armor of God. The belt of truth, the breastplate of righteousness, the shoes of the gospel, the helmet of salvation. I take up the shield of faith and the sword of the spirit, and I choose to be strong in the Lord and in the strength of Your might. I declare my dependence on You, and I take my stand against the enemy and all of his lying ways. I choose to believe the truth, and I refuse to be discouraged. You are the God of all hope, and I am confident that You will meet my every need.

I ask Your spirit to send people to pray for us. I now call forth the kingdom of God, throughout my home, my household, my kingdom and domain. In the authority of the Lord Jesus Christ. Giving all glory and honor and thanks to Him. In Jesus's name. Amen.

Moment Maker

You Can Live Your Life or It Will Live You

Carlos Whittaker

Every day we have an opportunity to make our lives meaningful, to make them matter. Yet, for so many of us, we let too much of life happen without taking notice.

Have you ever "killed time" while waiting for an appointment? How often do you watch the clock at the end of your shift?

When was the last time you stopped where you were and just savored life?

Choosing to make each moment count is the foundation of what it means to be a Moment Maker. And, for Carlos Whittaker, moment making is a part of everything he does.

Carlos guides people to moments with God in his role as a worship leader. He encourages others to make their own moments in his wildly popular blog. He has captured personal moments on video that have gone viral. Living deliberately—and teaching others to do so as well—is a way of life for Carlos.

In *Moment Maker*, Carlos shares moments from his own life that have formed his methodology for living on purpose and with purpose. As you will find in these pages, the beauty of having a moment-making life is that it does not require a big investment in time, energy, or money. It simply requires a commitment to pay attention.

All around you there are opportunities to meet a need, to shift your focus, and to begin healing. It is time to become a Moment Maker.